WILD WOMEN of BOSTON

WILD WOMEN

of BOSTON

Mettle and Moxie in the Hub

DINA VARGO

THE History PRESS

Published by The History Press
Charleston, SC 29403
www.historypress.net

Copyright © 2015 by Dina Vargo
All rights reserved

First published 2015

Manufactured in the United States

ISBN 978.1.62619.795.4

Library of Congress Control Number: 2015932920

To Mum and Dad
Thanks for all the family trips to Gettysburg and Williamsburg

For my original Wild Woman, Helen Junda

CONTENTS

CONTENTS

Acknowledgements

ppreciation, gratitude and countless thanks are in order for the many who helped me with this project. Let me start by thanking the entire Boston By Foot organization, led by Samantha Nelson, Veronika McDonald King and Boston's best volunteer tour guides. Thanks for creating a place for me to geek out on history.

Allow me to raise a glass of Madeira to my Graveyard Girls—Margaret Bratschi, Judy Glock, Gretchen Grozier and Heather Pence—for their encouragement, input and, above all, friendship.

There would be no book without the resources provided by the Boston Public Library, in particular Aaron Schmidt in the Print Department, as well as the American Antiquities Society; the Museum of Fine Arts, Boston; the Massachusetts Historical Society; and the Art Resource.

I'd like to also thank my commissioning editor at The History Press, Tabitha Dulla, for making this a smooth and enjoyable experience.

For the short time that I've known Malini Biswas, I'm especially indebted to her for her kindness, patience and home cooking. Thanks also to Michele Meltzer, who listened to my tales on our almost daily runs, and Sharon Callahan for her friendship and support.

Finally, I owe an enormous debt of gratitude and special thanks to Sally Ebeling, who provided invaluable guidance and editing advice. I am forever grateful.

INTRODUCTION

$\mathcal{W}$riting a *Wild Women of Boston* book would seem to be almost a no-brainer. There are countless female firebrands, matronly mavericks and rabble-rousing reformers throughout Boston's history who could literally fill a book, or two or three. For example:

The first African American poet in America's history? Phyllis Wheatley.

The only *Mayflower* passenger to make her way to Boston? Mary Chilton is buried in King's Chapel Cemetery.

The first African American female doctor and registered nurse? Rebecca Lee Crumpler and Mary Eliza Mahoney.

Writers of classic literature? Authors Louisa May Alcott and Harriet Beecher Stowe both wrote and lived in Boston.

Looking for the leader of the campaign to make Thanksgiving a national holiday? Give thanks to Sarah Josepha Hale.

Searching for suffragettes? My vote goes to Julia Ward Howe, Lucy Stone and Maud Wood Park.

Teachers of the blind? Annie Sullivan taught Helen Keller after being educated at the Perkins School for the Blind in South Boston.

Nobel Peace Prize winners, scientists, doctors and nurses. Architects, composers and artists. Writers and teachers. Collectors and patrons. Entrepreneurs. Abolitionists. Reformers. Boston has many women to be proud of. There is a Boston Women's Heritage Trail with no fewer than sixteen self-guided walks through almost as many Boston neighborhoods. Boston is not lacking in celebrating the impact of women on its history.

This, however, is not one of those books. Or at least not traditionally so.

Wild Women of Boston goes off the beaten path of the usual array of celebrated women. Although there is some overlap, *Wild Women* focuses on the outliers who don't get as much attention. Some of these women are perhaps better left unknown, like Alice Thomas, the Massachusetts Bay Madam. Nightmare Nurse "Jolly" Jane Toppan murdered so many people while claiming to care for them that she forgot how many exactly she'd killed. Rachel Wall was a thief and pirate. And even though Salem gets all the notoriety for trying witches, Boston hanged its fair share too.

Then there are those under-the-radar women like Elizabeth Murray and the Cuming sisters who were entrepreneurs in colonial Boston. Mercy Otis Warren did her job to galvanize the public in supporting independence from England in the run-up to the Revolutionary War. Sarah Parker Remond refused to be moved over one hundred years before Rosa Parks boarded a bus, and Kathrine Switzer ran her own "rogue" marathon in Boston.

Save the murderers, thieves and adulterers, many of these women had a lot in common. None of them really set out to be mavericks—well, except for Isabella Stewart Gardner, who was a natural at thumbing her nose at Boston's elite while they had no choice but to bow to her wishes. Most of these women found themselves in extraordinary circumstances and had the fortitude to meet their challenges head on. They by and large claimed no wish or need for the spotlight. One can picture Mary Brown Patten shrinking after being lionized in the newspapers after she piloted a clipper ship around Cape Horn in the stormiest of winter seasons. She died in practical anonymity, and she wanted it that way. Others were concerned about not stepping out of proscribed boundaries; Mercy Otis Warren in part wrote anonymously because her writing would not have carried the weight that it did if people knew she was a woman. Harriet Hemenway and Minna Hall put the leadership of the Audubon Society in the hands of men, knowing they faced the same problem as Mercy. And that was over one hundred years later! And our most modern of Boston's wild women sits quietly by the sea, secure in the fact that she got her job as the nation's first and only female U.S. Coast Guard lighthouse keeper because she was the best person for it. Have we come a long way, baby? There's hope yet.

There are most likely countless additional stories that are waiting to be told and stories that are still being made every day. Carry on, wild women of Boston!

Chapter 1

WITCHES AMONG US

Ann Hibbens and Goody Glover

*I*magine calling a contractor to do some work around your house. It may have taken some time and effort to get the contractor's quote, and it may have taken making multiple calls to multiple contractors (for some reason, this is never easy!). But finally you hire a contractor for your prescribed scope of work and price, and then you proceed. The contractor's work is fine but unfinished. Promises are made to come back to complete the job. Still, the invoice arrives at double the amount of the quote. The work is unfinished! The price is too high! What do you do?

Nowadays, you would make no bones about calling the contractor and arguing the point of paying when the work is complete. You would argue for the agreed-upon price. If you weren't satisfied, you might call the Better Business Bureau to file a complaint. In your frustration, you might put a negative review of the contractor on a website. You might even go to court. Taking these any of these actions are well within your twenty-first-century rights. But a woman in the 1650s who did something similar and publicly asserted herself risked being excommunicated from her church and maybe even hanged for witchcraft.

The modern homeowning scenario, relatively common today, has a history at least as far back as the 1650s. In 1656, Ann Hibbens expressed her frustration with a contractor publicly and tried to negotiate a fair price on a contract. For her efforts, she was tried and hanged for witchcraft in Boston.

Ann Hibbens

Ann and her husband were some of Boston's first settlers, arriving in the 1630s. By the 1640s, Ann's husband, a prosperous merchant, was becoming an important local player in the town's elected leadership. It was also around this time that the Hibbens family had some work done at their home by a carpenter. Ann felt that the family was grossly overcharged and cheated. She did not take this lying down; she made her feelings known publicly. Considering the population of Boston in 1640 was approximately 1,200 people, there were few who didn't hear about Ann's crusade against the contractor. Rather than gaining support for her cause, she actually came off as a harridan, causing a lot of discomfort among the townspeople. As a woman living in colonial times, by seeking a remedy to her family's problem and doing it in a very public way, she overstepped social boundaries, and the community turned against her in a very big way.

First, in 1640, she was censured by the First Church of Boston, Boston's oldest and most exclusive church, in a bitter trial. For her "turbulent passion" in seeking damages from the carpenter, she was charged with "transgressing the rule of the Apostle"—basically, she was charged with overstepping her husband's authority. Church members felt that she'd misbehaved and embarrassed her husband—an ugly offense. What's worse, she refused to apologize, which led to her excommunication from the church for being unrepentant.

When Thomas Hutchinson wrote about the event in his *History of the Colony and Province of Massachusetts Bay* in 1764, he surmised that several bad business decisions Ann's husband had made, with consequent loss of cash, "increased [her] natural crabbedness," which in turn made her "turbulent and quarrelsome." This quarrelsome behavior came out one afternoon as Ann, walking into town, saw two women whispering to each other. She confronted them and wanted to know if they were talking about her. Big surprise, they were! How would she know such a thing? Perhaps because she was the talk of the town, but no matter, suspicions of her precognitive abilities were raised.

She became a pariah in Boston. When her husband died of old age in 1654, the floodgates of accusations against her opened. In 1655, she was tried for witchcraft.

The case against her was flimsy, at best. As was the custom, her body was searched for "witches' teats," an extra teat from which an imp or familiar would suckle human blood, and none was found. The so-called extra teat

This illustration depicts the execution of Ann Hibbens on Boston Common. It was published in 1886 in a book called *Lynn and Surroundings* by Clarence W. Hobbs.

could have been anything from an actual extra nipple to something as simple and ordinary as a skin tag, a mole or any sort of blemish. A search of her house for poppets or any small hint of performing witchcraft also turned up nothing. This may be why magistrates ruled in her favor during an initial trial. Public sentiment, however, demanded a retrial, and it was no surprise, not even to Ann, when the general court reversed the initial court's finding and condemned her to hang for witchcraft.

Ann maintained her innocence but accepted her fate, putting her estate in order. In June 1656, she met the hangman's noose. She wouldn't be the first to be hanged in Boston for witchcraft, and she wouldn't be the last.

IT'S WITCHCRAFT

While accusations of witchcraft in colonial Boston weren't common, they weren't unheard of, either. Even before the Salem witch trials in 1692, in New England alone, there were more than one hundred people accused of witchcraft.

The belief in witchcraft was a direct transfer from the settlers' lives in England. Up and down the Atlantic coast, there were witchcraft accusations in each of the colonies of the New World. However, in New England, these accusations were far more numerous and taken far more seriously. This was due to the more conservative viewpoint of the Puritans compared to their colonial counterparts and the Puritanical obsession with making the world a more ordered and orderly place to live. When people talk about Puritans today, they use terms like "strict," "rigid," "prim and proper" and "austere." All of these descriptions have a basis in history—Puritans were obsessed with controlling their world, and if a perceived "devil" was interfering with that goal, then the devil must be rooted out. This was serious business.

Witchcraft was also very real, although today we wouldn't call it witchcraft, we'd call it superstition. More specifically, counter-magic was practiced in daily life in colonial New England. This was not meant to be hurtful; it was used more for protection. Our wintertime evergreen wreath on the front door was yesterday's magic for warding away evil spirits. Similarly, hanging a horseshoe over a doorway served the same purpose. Fortunately, most of us no longer fill bottles with our urine; then add nails, pins, hair and fingernail clippings; and bury them under the hearth for protection. In the same vein, reading fortunes by mixing up egg whites, asking a question of a mirror in the candlelight or reading the letters formed by discarded apple skins might be a popular activity among the slumber party set today. These practices were more prevalent in colonial New England—again, another way of controlling the environment—but the line between counter-magic and witchcraft was a fine one. If persons accused of witchcraft were found to have dabbled at all in counter-magic, the case against them was stronger.

THE ACCUSED

But why were people accused to begin with? What brought on accusations of witchcraft? By and large, these accusations were made after a dispute among neighbors, were generally worked out in the minor courts and may have resulted in payment of a fine or some other negligible punishment. Men could be accused as well as women. However, occasionally, the accusations resulted in a full-blown trial for witchcraft, and when that happened, the accused routinely had several things in common.

First, they were women. Women were accused at least four times more often than men, and when men were accused, they received less severe punishment. In Boston, no men were ever accused of, much less executed for, witchcraft. In colonial New England, women were considered to be inferior, weaker and more easily corruptible by Satan.

They might have been healers or used *physick*. They were considered healers if their concoctions worked and witches if they didn't.

Often, they were alone in the world, probably widowed. They were middle-aged or older, beyond their childbearing years and, thus, of no further use to society. They might have also had fewer children or even no children—again, another display of their inferiority.

They were usually poor, although Ann Hibbens is the odd exception to the rule; her family was influential, and her standing in society was much higher than the average witch. However, her strong will—another trait common among the accused—acted against her and certainly branded her a troublemaker.

And it's trouble with a capital "T" that the Witch Glover stirred up in 1688.

Goody Glover

John and Martha Goodwin were beside themselves with fear and confusion. Days before, their children—Martha, thirteen years old; John, eleven; Mercy, seven; and Benjamin, five—had all been acting strangely. They barked like dogs. They purred like cats. They screwed up their bodies in painful contortions and screamed out in pain. Their tongues hung out of their mouths onto their chins or were pulled deep into their throats. What on earth was happening? Clearly, they were bewitched. And the only person who could have done it, everyone knew, was the old crone Goody Glover.

Goody Glover was an elderly widow who, ever since her arrival in Boston from Ireland (by way of Barbados, where she'd been sold as a servant), had developed a nasty reputation. Just weeks earlier, the younger Martha Goodwin accused Goody's daughter, a laundress for the family, of stealing an article of clothing. Goody would have none of it, confronting the child directly, using very bad language. Soon after, Martha started to have strange fits. Then, her siblings began to suffer the same bone-cracking afflictions.

John Goodwin had no idea what to do, thinking only of protecting his family. When the doctors could do nothing for his kids, he consulted the chief religious leaders in Boston, who quickly took charge by holding a prayer vigil that released the youngest, Benjamin, from the spell.

A neighborhood investigation quickly closed in on Goody, who never denied her role in the drama. She actually dug herself in deeper by her belligerent behavior, and she was jailed. When she was asked if she believed in God, Cotton Mather said that "her answer was too blasphemous and horrible for any pen of mine to mention."

She didn't make it easy for authorities. When it was determined that a full trial was needed to suss out what exactly was going on, she wasn't at all cooperative. She chose to speak in Gaelic, rather than English, and demanded that it be translated.

Authorities also found "poppets" while searching her home. Poppets were small dolls made of rags that acted something like voodoo dolls. These poppets enabled Goody to control the objects of her enchantments, which she showed the full court in a horrifying reenactment. She spat on her fingers, and as she rubbed them over the body of the poppets, the Goodwin children attending court that day writhed in pain, screaming out and begging Goody to stop.

It was also during the trial that more information about Goody's past came to light. A woman named Mrs. Hughes felt compelled to tell the court about an encounter her dying neighbor had with Goody some years before. The neighbor explained to Mrs. Hughes that Goody was responsible for her very death. But before Mrs. Hughes could even take the stand, her son mysteriously took ill after, he swore, he saw Goody creep into his room late at night and attempt to disembowel him. Mrs. Hughes confronted Goody while she was in jail, and Goody confessed to the deed, acting out in anger against those who had accused her. Mrs. Hughes begged Goody to release her son from the enchantment, and Goody agreed. Mrs. Hughes's son quickly recovered.

That small act of kindness could not help Goody Glover. She was hanged in Boston on November 16, 1688. Before they threw the noose around her neck, she told onlookers that her hanging would not alleviate the terrors of the Goodwin children because there were others like her out there who were also involved. And she was right; the children continued to be vexed by their pains and wild behavior. If there were co-conspirators, no one ever found out who they were, but after several weeks and many prayers, the children were finally released from their tormentor, Goody Glover.

Chapter 2

THE DIVORCEE AND THE MASSACHUSETTS BAY MADAM

Katherine Nanny Naylor and Alice Thomas

The Wheelwright family of Massachusetts would not let the matter rest. One of the oldest and most established families in the Massachusetts Bay Colony would not let the name of their kin be sullied, most especially not by a common trollop. Katherine had been through enough, what with the abuse she and her children had suffered. Although they'd rid themselves of that miscreant of a husband, the fact was that the madam with whom he was intimately acquainted refused to give up her client list. That was an insult they wouldn't let her get away with. The Wheelwrights would make sure that their family would not be the only ones to bear the brunt of this public embarrassment. They would bring down Alice Thomas too. Wheelwright would not be the only name dragged through the dirt. Appropriately so, because this is where this story resurfaced—in the dirt. It was a team of archaeologists who dug up this colonial drama.

THE LITTLE DIG

The Central Artery Project was the largest and most complex transportation construction project that has been completed to date in the United States. Beginning in 1991, the project did away with a dull green-painted elevated highway and replaced it with a system of buried highways, mass transit,

This straight pin found in Katherine Nanny Naylor's privy is made of copper. It was likely a part of her sewing kit. *Courtesy of the Massachusetts Historical Commission.*

bridges and tunnels. It was a feat of both innovative engineering and wild cost overages. The project, locally called the Big Dig, took roughly fifteen years to complete and changed the skyline and landscape of Boston forever. Bostonians endured almost constant noise, traffic snarls and the inconvenience that only a $22 billion project can bring. But there were "little digs" going on as well.

Major construction projects that receive federal funding must plan for the impact on historic sites, and in an old place like Boston, this called for several archaeological digs to be undertaken in several places around the city. When the team of archaeologists excavated a site in Boston's North End, they hit pay dirt. They struck upon a privy that was filled in with trash. Under normal circumstances, this may not sound particularly enticing—finding an outhouse filled with rubbish—but archaeologists know better. The artifacts they found at the Cross Street dig told a bigger story about everyday life, lived by everyday people, in colonial Boston.

When they started to piece together the meaning of their cache of shoes, glass, pottery, clothing fasteners and even a wooden bowling ball, details of a life lived hundreds of years ago emerged. Digging deeper into court records, diaries and newspaper reports, historians uncovered the dramatic story of a colonial woman befitting a movie on the Lifetime network. How the privileged but personally troubled life of Katherine Nanny Naylor intersected with one of Boston's early wild women, the enterprising if immoral Alice Thomas, proved to be life changing for both of them.

THE DIVORCEE

Katherine Wheelwright Nanny arrived in Boston as a five-year-old girl in 1635. Her father was a well-respected reverend until he cleaved a little too closely to the opinions of his sister-in-law, Anne Hutchinson, a wild woman in her own right. Anne had a different way of thinking about Puritan ideology that rubbed the established clergy the wrong way, and her views were so popular that she developed a following. A woman with opposing views *and* devotees? That wouldn't stand in Puritan Boston. She was tried and banished from the town. The Wheelwright family was banished for their heretical beliefs, moving from Exeter, New Hampshire; to Wells, Maine; to Salisbury, Massachusetts; and eventually back to Exeter again in the years following. Sometime between 1646 and 1653, Katherine married a merchant named Robert Nanny, who was seventeen years her senior. The two lived on Ann Street in Boston's North End and had eight children together, only two of whom survived childhood. In 1663, Robert Nanny died, leaving his North End property to his children but to be held in trust by Katherine.

By 1666, Katherine had met and married Edward Naylor, another merchant. That's when the trouble started. They had two children, but soon after the birth of the second child, Naylor was shown to be not only a cheater but also viciously abusive to both Katherine and their children. By 1671, Katherine had petitioned the superior court for divorce on the grounds of adultery and abuse.

Divorce, while never a preferred course of action in colonial Massachusetts, wasn't necessarily uncommon or impossible to achieve. Divorce laws were transferred to the colonies from England, but it was surprisingly easier to get a divorce in Puritan Massachusetts than in England or anywhere else in the colonies. Puritans recognized marriage and divorce as civil, not religious, contracts. Anglicans thought differently. They believed the marriage contract was essentially religiously and legally unbreakable. Still, it wasn't easy or desirable to divorce in New England. A petitioner needed to prove that adultery, desertion or cruelty had

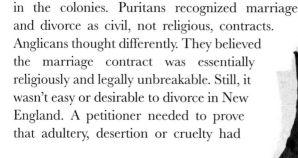

This child's shoe was found in the Cross Street archaeology dig. It is one of the earliest examples of American-made footwear. *Courtesy of the Massachusetts Historical Commission.*

taken place. Eyewitnesses needed to testify, and proof of extreme bodily harm needed to be brought to court. Women rarely brought complaints to court and even more rarely were successful in being granted divorces. A situation would have to be drastic to bring one's private life out into the public realm and hold it out for public criticism. Katherine's circumstances were desperate.

The safety of Katherine's family was at risk, as well as her own life. It was reported that just days after she gave birth to one of their children, Naylor dragged Katherine out of bed against her will for the superficial social task of visiting their neighbors. Servants attested to how Naylor threw plates and chairs at Katherine and other members of the family. At one point, after waiting for Naylor to come home late one evening— where he was, only God knew—Katherine served her husband dinner that she'd kept warm. Not good enough! He pitched it across the room and then demanded a new meal. Servants also reported seeing Naylor throw one of his infant children to the floor and kick another down a set of stairs.

If this mental and physical abuse wasn't enough, Naylor also had a long string of dalliances with other women. He made passes at servants in his own home who refused him. He also made passes at servants who didn't refuse him;

Artist John Mackie Falconer's depiction of 78 Cross Street, Boston, near where Katherine Nanny Naylor lived. *Courtesy of the National Gallery of Art, Reba and Dave Williams Collection.*

Mary Read was carrying his baby. Mary Read was a jealous lover who made Katherine pay for her envy. Katherine recounted for the court how she felt ill after drinking a beer. Later, it came to light that Mary Read had procured a bit of henbane, an extremely toxic plant. Katherine had been poisoned. But it was Naylor's affair with Mary Moore that would prove disastrous.

Neighbors reported seeing Naylor cavorting with Mary Moore and others in several different establishments, one of which was a notorious brothel owned by Alice Thomas, the first madam in Massachusetts.

THE MASSACHUSETTS BAY MADAM

Alice Thomas was an everyday Puritan housewife until her husband died, and then, left without any financial support, she had to find a way to make ends meet. She owned a shop, but it didn't cover her bills. She became a prostitute to augment her income and wound up becoming so much more than that. She started to work with other prostitutes, coordinating their activities and customers, becoming Massachusetts's first madam. Unfortunately, one of her clients was Edward Naylor. And one of her "employees" was Mary Moore.

As the Naylor divorce case was being heard in court, a neighbor came forward to attest to seeing Naylor and Mary Moore several times in Alice's establishment. In fact, he had seen a transaction take place as he peeped through Alice's window. Alice was held accountable for Naylor's actions as an adulterer; it was alleged she provided ample and easy opportunity for Naylor to satisfy his illegal urges. Alice was thrown into jail in January 1672. She was charged with theft and "frequent secret and unseasonable entertainment in her house to lewd, lascivious and notorious persons of both sexes, giving them opportunities to commit carnal wickedness."

The punishment, made certain by the influential Wheelwright family, did not suit the crime by today's standards. The family felt they had suffered enough embarrassment; they blamed Alice for bringing the family so low. She was dragged through the streets to the gallows with a noose around her neck. While the court decided whether she would hang, she was readied for the gallows and made to stand on the threshold to wait for the hangman to knock the platform out from under her. Having sweated that out for over an hour, all the time wondering if her next breath would be her last, she was stripped to bare her back and breasts and was lashed thirty-nine painful times until her shoulders were a bloody mess. While she lay shivering in a heap on the ground, townspeople came to hurl insults, snow and ice at her. She was taken back to the jail, where she served out her sentence of nine months. After that, she was driven out of Boston and told to never return. That would be the end of the story—except that Alice returned.

Perhaps to redeem herself in the eyes of the community, Alice Thomas did not leave Boston forever. Four years after her banishment, she used her substantial savings, ill gotten though they were, to contribute to the growing town. There seemed to be no objections to accepting her generous gifts by those in charge—the same men who ordered her stripped, whipped and cast out. Despite all that, she made donations to the building of a sea wall and to other public buildings. Because of her good deeds and sizable cash contributions, she was able to petition the court and won a repeal of her order to exile in 1676.

That very sea wall or the foundation of a building Alice helped finance could be buried at our feet, waiting to be uncovered by some other archaeologist on some other project. Who knows what stories remain untold?

Chapter 3
WAR OF WORDS

Mercy Otis Warren

As the British took up residence in Boston during the siege of the town from April 1775 to March 1776, they needed to break the monotony of life marooned on the Shawmut Peninsula (today's downtown Boston). The winter was brutal and long. Food was scarce, and simple supplies were hard to get; winter storms in the Atlantic, an iced-over harbor and opportunistic privateers made delivering provisions extremely hard. Keeping warm was an ongoing concern. Buildings were torn apart for firewood, including the Second Church of Boston, popularly known then as the Old North Meeting House, where the Mathers presided. The Liberty Tree, a famous elm tree around which the Sons of Liberty would gather, produced a fair amount of cordwood. Life was hard for the British soldiers and those civilians who remained in Boston. But life was a lot less tough for the British gentry, who saw fit to create a social season for themselves.

Balls, dinners and other entertainments were provided for the British officers and their wives. On the evening of January 8, 1776, a special event was planned. Faneuil Hall was turned into a theater—a major affront to Bostonians, who had made attending the theater illegal in 1642—and the well-to-do came out in their finest dress to attend. The play was called *The Blockade*. It was written as a farce by General John Burgoyne, who would, in October 1777, be handed a major defeat by the Continental army at Saratoga. General Burgoyne, besides being a celebrated soldier who proved himself in the French and Indian War, was an accomplished playwright. *The Blockade* was meant to ridicule the Patriots and the war they were waging against a far superior British force. The play made special fun of General George Washington, who it depicted in a massive white wig, dragging a rusty sword.

The crowd settled in to laugh and join in the fun at the expense of the foolish and fearful Patriots, but they didn't know that their opponent had two secret weapons: one was the cannonade about to go off during the play, and the second was the pen of Mercy Otis Warren.

At first, the cannon fire the audience heard was assumed to be a clever part of the play, and they applauded appreciatively. But when General Howe cried "Turn out! Turn out!" it was quickly apparent that the joke was on the gentry.

Mercy Otis Warren would also join in on the joke when she turned the play *The Blockade* into her very own farce called *The Blockheads*, a searing takedown of the British and a call to arms for the Revolution. This was one of several satires she anonymously wrote that were published in the Boston presses. She helped to galvanize support for the Revolution and for the values of the early republic. Later, she'd take on the monumental work of writing a three-volume history of the Revolution, which caused a major rift in her friendship with John Adams, and she occasionally became the center of criticism herself. Who would ever guess that this middle-aged mother of five would become a pivotal propagandist, serving as a messenger of Revolutionary thought? And who would have thought that the same woman would enter a bitter war of words with one of her closest friends, her earliest supporter and former president of the United States, John Adams?

Beginnings

Mercy Otis Warren was born in the town of West Barnstable on Cape Cod in 1728. She was very well educated for a female; although it might have been proper for her to be able to write and read Bible verses, her level of education went far beyond that. Fortuitously for Mercy, her intelligence was recognized and cultivated by her father. In an unusual move for the times, he allowed her to study along with her brothers, who were being prepared for Harvard. Both her father, James Otis Sr., and brother, James Otis Jr., were staunch opponents of the British, whom they considered to be too involved in colonial affairs. Her brother famously led the defense against the Writs of Assistance, a sort of blanket search warrant that was too easily abused by British custom officials, in court, and many think he coined the phrase "taxation without representation is tyranny." For the Otis family, their opposition was also personal—James Sr. had been passed over for appointment as chief of superior court for the better-connected Thomas Hutchinson. Hutchinson would, in turn, become a major focus of Mercy's ire in her later satirical writings.

Because of the involvement of her father and brother in the formative years of republican thinking, the home that Mercy shared with her husband, James Warren, in Plymouth, Massachusetts, became a hub of Revolutionary thought. As the political situation worsened, it became a sort of salon for Patriot discussion and planning that attracted other Patriot leaders, like John Adams and Samuel Adams. It quickly evolved into a hotbed where Mercy joined discussions, traded ideas and sharpened her opinions. Although it would not have been appropriate for her to take part in political conversations in more traditional households, she was a highly intellectual woman who formed her own opinions, and she wasn't afraid to share them—at least privately, among friends.

MERCY TAKES UP HER PEN

Mercy wrote poetry privately, for herself and her friends, but her talent was soon requested for the Revolution. As her husband became more publicly involved in the run-up to the Revolution, he served as the chairman of the Plymouth Committee of Correspondence and, with Samuel Adams, wrote the Solemn League and Covenant that called for a complete boycott of British goods. To this end, Mercy weighed in, writing a poem focusing on the role that women could play, encouraging them to forgo buying British-made fashion items. This she called "The Vanities of Life." (This would eventually hurt two other of our wild women, Ame and Elizabeth Cuming.)

In 1772, Mercy wrote a play, *The Adulateur.* She took direct aim at Thomas Hutchinson, who by then was the governor of Massachusetts. Despite being a native-born resident of Massachusetts, many saw him as no better than the mouthpiece and sycophant of the King who used the law of the land to his and his family's own benefit. The other characters in the play represented real political players to whom she gave outrageous names like Crusty Crowbar, Brigadier Hateall, Dupe, Simple Sapling, Hum Humbug and Sir Sparrow Spendall. Another wild woman, Elizabeth Lloyd Loring, was re-cast as Mrs. Flourish, which may not sound too damning to our ears now, but then the word "flourish" was a slang term for sexual intercourse. Clearly, no one was safe from the wrath of Mercy's pen.

The Adulateur was so appreciated among supporters of the Patriot cause that they started to refer to the actual people by Mercy's chosen names for them in her play—for instance, Thomas Hutchinson was referred to as his fictional doppelganger, Rapatio.

She went on to write *The Defeat*, *The Group* and, later, *The Blockheads*, to public approval and acclaim. Each piece pushed further, painting British and Loyalists ever darker and making clear that the true heroes were the Patriots. These parts were played in real time by her brother, husband and other friends.

A portrait of Mercy Otis Warren as depicted in the book *Eminent Americans*, written in 1886 by John Benson Lossing. *Courtesy of the Internet Book Archive Database.*

Mercy, it should be said, wrote all these pieces anonymously, not because she wanted to hide behind her words but for reasons both social and practical. Practically speaking, many others wrote anonymously at the time, if only not to be jailed for their treasonous views. Writing anonymously or with a pen name was not uncommon. It is thought that Samuel Adams wrote a dramatized account of the Boston Massacre anonymously, and even Thomas Paine's famous pamphlet, *Common Sense*, was published anonymously when it was first made available in the colonies. Both of these writings had the effect of galvanizing colonists to the cause against Britain and, eventually, to full independence from Britain. But Mercy was first and foremost a woman. She knew that she was stepping outside societal boundaries anytime she picked up her pen and had her work published. She did not wish to upset the social apple cart by revealing that she was female, and ultimately, she "knew her place" and was comfortable staying out of the limelight. However, those in the know were absolutely certain that Mercy was behind the writings. She would take full credit for them later in life because, unfortunately, others would take credit for themselves.

Many attributed her 1788 *Observations on the New Constitution* to Elbridge Gerry, who helped distribute the work. He was also a strong anti-Federalist (he went so far as to refuse to sign the new Constitution because it granted too much power to a centralized government). Other readers attributed the work to Mercy's husband. Insightfully, she advocated for a Bill of Rights, which would, as we know, eventually come to pass. Her anti-Federalist views, however, put her friendship with John and Abigail Adams in conflict, bringing their years of collaboration and mutual support to a stormy end.

MERCY AND THE ADAMS FAMILY

John Adams was one of Mercy's biggest and earliest supporters. He asked her to write a poem in the aftermath of the Boston Tea Party. She readily supplied a piece cheekily called "The Squabble of the Sea Nymphs." Adams arranged for the poem to be printed on the front page of the *Boston Gazette* in March 1774. The poem featured the goings-on of Neptune, Amphytrite, Proteus and Salacia, sea gods and goddesses who were eager to grab a cuppa, and the heroic doings of our Patriots:

> *Resolv'd to set the western world on fire,*
> *By scattering the weed of Indian shores;*
> *Or worse, to lodge it in Pygmalion's shores:*
> *But if the artifice should not succeed,*
> *Then, in revenge, attempt some bolder deed;*
> *For while old ocean's mighty billows roar,*
> *Or foaming surges lash the distant shore,*
> *Shall goddesses regale like woodland dames?*
> *First let Chinesan herbage feed the flames.*

It was often John Adams's approval she sought for any of her satirical plays, and he was pleased to indulge her. But as Mercy's husband took on a greater role during the Revolution, Mercy divided her time between their Plymouth home and her husband's headquarters just outside Boston. It was during this time she developed a close friendship with Abigail Adams. Both were effectively war widows, if in name only, because their husbands were so often absent from their homes. They were also committed to the cause—what greater sacrifice could they make than giving up their husbands to the war?

WAR OF WORDS

A search of your local bookstore today would reveal that most works of history are still written by men. Consider, then, the year 1805, when Mercy published a three-volume history of the American Revolution. This time, she took credit for her work under her own name.

To write the book, she requested letters and other public documents, and she interviewed the major players involved in bringing our fledgling country through the war, including John Adams and Elbridge Gerry. She also used her personal recollections of conversations she participated in prior to the war and those she was party to as her husband's secretary. Called *History of the Rise, Progress and Termination of the American Revolution*, her history was different from the other histories written at the same time. She focused less on military history, instead writing a social history. She wrote of the efforts of the Founding Fathers, but she also highlighted efforts of regular citizens, especially women. While male writers ignored the less-than-honorable behavior of the military, Mercy called it out and wrote specifically of instances of women being taken advantage of or, worse, assaulted and raped. The book was well received, but two other titles, having appeared just before hers, stole her thunder.

She believed that her role as a historian was, in part, to comment on the character of the main actors. She took aim at her friend John Adams, possibly as a personal attack because of their disagreement over the direction of the new United States Constitution. He was a strong Federalist; she was not. She accused him of being an ineffective ambassador to England because he let himself be caught up in the pomp and majesty of the gilded halls of the monarchy. She believed that he had lost touch with the republican ideals he had trumpeted prior to and during the Revolution. This caused an all-out war of words with Adams, which culminated in no fewer than sixteen letters exchanged between the two over the course of the summer of 1807. He defended his record, and she, insulted, maintained her views. This caused a five-year silence between the two, which went unabated even as their friends tried to intercede.

Adams's response was personal. He attacked not just her words but also the fact that she was a woman, as though he was more insulted by her femaleness than by her actual opinions. In more than 1,200 pages, in three volumes, she spent very few words on Adams—which was perhaps even more insulting! In her view, she spoke well of him in general but didn't hold back in criticizing him when she believed it necessary. As she defended herself, she responded rationally, but she refused to back down. She invited Adams to write his own history of the Revolution!

Adams had reason to be upset. John and Abigail Adams had been perhaps the greatest source of encouragement for her writing. John sent her accounts of his travels and works during the Revolution, giving her practically a front-row seat at the show. Abigail also shared her letters from John with Mercy. Although Mercy took a less personal, more professional tone with Adams in the defense of her words, she had likely been affected by her personal acrimony while writing *History*. Edith B. Geddes, a biographer of Abigail Adams, posits that their bitter correspondence actually cemented the reputation of John Adams forever in history of being a curmudgeonly and ego-driven Founder.

As Mercy came to terms with the end of the friendship, she received some additional criticism of her work. The criticism seemed to take clear aim at the fact that she was a female historian. A writer in a journal called *The Pamphlet* observed that the book came from "a mind that had not yielded to the assertion that all political attentions lay outside the road of female life." Had she written the book anonymously, or had the credit been given to a man, would the same criticism have been leveled? If she had not written anonymously in the past, would her works have been dismissed as coming from the uninformed female mind? Perhaps it was better, then, that she took credit later; otherwise, her writing avocation may have been cut short.

CLOSING CHAPTER

Mercy died at the age of eighty-six on October 19, 1814, after mending fences with John Adams two years prior. She is buried at Burial Hill in Plymouth, Massachusetts. Her history is considered to be the first of the American Revolution to be written by a woman and, perhaps even more importantly, the only history to be written by an eyewitness, male or female.

Chapter 4
MERCHANT OF THE SHE

Elizabeth Murray

Elizabeth's marriage hadn't been a mistake. At least, her choice of spouse wasn't a mistake. It was the institution of marriage that put her at a distinct disadvantage. Thomas Campbell was everything a woman could want in a husband. He was a successful merchant. He and Elizabeth's family had known each other from their days in North Carolina, where Thomas's shipping fleet was based. The two were also Scottish, born if not raised. No, the man wasn't the problem. But the institution of marriage, with its meaning for women in the colonial era—that was the sticking point. It was a problem that left her nearly destitute. She'd learned a vital lesson, though. It wasn't a mistake she'd make in her second marriage or in her third marriage, for that matter. Today, some might consider her cunning or even a gold digger. Elizabeth was neither of those things. Elizabeth was smart, and she wouldn't again lose her fortune, the one she had built from the ground up almost entirely by herself. She'd defend her home and estate against British and rebel soldiers alike. She'd also ensure the security of her financial life by having all of her subsequent husbands sign prenuptial agreements. It was hardly a familiar (in fact, an almost unheard of) concept at the time.

INDEPENDENT WOMAN

Elizabeth Murray was born in Scotland and traveled to North Carolina to be her older brother's housekeeper at the age of twelve in 1739. For a short time, Elizabeth managed her brother James's estate in North Carolina before the family moved again, this time to London. There, she was exposed to a large cosmopolitan city that was not only fashionable but also had its share of shops owned and operated by women. By 1749, the family was on the move again, returning to the colonies. On their way back to North Carolina, they stopped in Boston, and Elizabeth never left.

ELIZABETH MURRAY,

Next 'Door to Deacon Bouteneau's *in Cornhill,* Boston, TEACHES *Drefden,* and other kinds of Needle Works, likewife accommodates young Ladies with Board, and half Board, at a reafonable Price ; fells flowered and clear Lawns, Cambricks, Muflins, Gauze, neweft Fafhion Caps, Ruffles, Tippits, Stomachers, Solitairs, Necklaces, Ear Rings, Ivory, Ebony and Bone Stick Fans, Women's Shoes, Stockings, Gloves and Mittens, Canvas, Crewils, Flofs, Flowering and Nuns Threads, Needles, Pins and Tapes, with fundry other Articles.

TO BE SOLD *at No.* 5 *on the Long Wharf, a parcel of new Cordage, and an Anchor of about* 900 *weight, alfo choice barrel'd Beef, very cheap for the Cafh.*

CHOICE Lifbon *Salt on board the Snow* Welcome, Matthew Cadwell, *Mafter, lying in the Harbour, to be fold by* Timothy Fitch.

TO BE LET,

BY Elizabeth Grice, *at the lower End of Waterftreet, a Copper that will boil off* 3 *Barrels and an half of Soap.*

CHoice fcrew'd HAY, to be fold at Mr. *Cradock's* Wharf, at the South End.

STRONG BEER, *or* MALT *for thofe who incline to brew it themfelves; to be fold by* Samuel Adams, *at a very reafonable Rate.*

TO be fold oppofite the Elm Trees at the South End, at the Sign of the Glove and Sugar Loaf, a Quantity of dry fweet Marjoram, likewife a choice parcel of Garden Seeds, faved the laft Year, by the Perfon himfelf from the beft of Plants, and where may be had good *Englifh* early Cabbage Seed, and in the Seafon of it, early Plants of feveral Sorts.

Bofton, Printed and fold by *T. Fleet* at the Heart and Crown in Cornhill

This advertisement for Elizabeth Murray's shop lists the shop location and offers embroidery lessons. The ad ran in the March 25, 1751 edition of the *Boston Evening-Post. Courtesy of the American Antiquarian Society.*

Why did she stay? We have no idea what went through twenty-three-year-old Elizabeth's mind in 1749 to make this daring decision to stay in an unknown city by herself, with her family hundreds of miles away. Her options were limited; she was too educated to become a housemaid, yet so many other possibilities were closed to her because she was a woman. It was a man's world; a woman could really only go so far as her husband would allow her. She had very few rights, much less an identity. Still, Elizabeth decided to go into the millinery business and strike out on her own in Boston. This decision is all the more remarkable in that her family supported her decision, both in word and deed—they gave her the financial backing she needed to start her endeavor. And their money wasn't ill spent. They got a return on their investment, as Elizabeth would in later years offer her two brothers financial support and a base of business in Boston with the contacts that she'd made.

Setting up shop wasn't easy. It was as much about establishing a reputation as it was gaining credit. But with the help of her merchant brothers, she managed to stock her shop with the latest fashions from London. And when stock was depleted, she put empty cartons on the shelves to disguise that fact. She never let them see her sweat, and she learned some tough lessons about the competitive nature of the business. She augmented her income by teaching young women needlework. She was ahead of schedule on paying her debts. She took trips to London to choose her own inventory to ensure that her shop would carry the latest trends to appeal to her Bostonian customers. When her business and business reputation were at last established, it was time to think about having a family.

AN INSTITUTE YOU CAN'T DISPARAGE

When Elizabeth Murray married Thomas Campbell, there was no modern-era notion that it would be forever. That just wasn't the reality of colonial America. The death of a child or a spouse was a sad and unfortunate fact of life. Certainly, Elizabeth did not hesitate to join finances with her husband. It wasn't that she really had any alternative. According to law, all that Elizabeth brought to the marriage was now Thomas's and would be even after his death. Married women had no right to enter into or make contracts, which included wills. They were not allowed to own property. There was no protection of a woman's finances independent of her husband. So, despite the decade of owning and managing her own shop from the ground up and becoming, if not independently wealthy, at least independently able to make ends meet, all the fruits of her labor became her husband's upon marriage. Because Elizabeth did not intend to quit working, and neither did Thomas, they combined resources and split responsibilities. For three years, the two happily lived, ran their businesses and were excited to announce that their family would soon increase by one. And then, tragedy struck. Then, it struck again.

First, a measles outbreak claimed the life of Thomas. Soon after, Elizabeth either miscarried or lost her baby at childbirth. These losses were devastating in their own right, but adding insult to injury was the loss of her financial stability. Her husband's family accused Elizabeth of wrongly accounting their finances as she settled his estate. Still, she had the shop and the confidence in her ability to carry on. Marriage was the last thing on her mind as she resolved to start again and considered life alone. When the prospect of marrying again did arise, she found the right man. And this man wanted to do right by her.

Only a year after being widowed, she was being courted by another Scotsman, this one almost forty years her senior. She resisted at first, but her family in North Carolina convinced her to reconsider. James Smith was rich, rich, rich. And not only that, he was so in love with Elizabeth that he did something very much out of the ordinary. He agreed to sign a prenuptial agreement giving Elizabeth a great portion of his wealth upon his death and granting her legal rights not normally given to women.

With the marriage agreement in 1760, Elizabeth became a wildly wealthy woman. She moved into another phase of her career, that of mistress of an estate, benefactress and mentor. She moved from living atop her shop on Queen Street in downtown Boston to Smith's estate in Brush Hill in Milton, Massachusetts. There she would oversee and encourage the careers of several young she-merchants.

No longer needing to work, she decided to stay busy and productive by spreading her wealth—both her material wealth and her wealth of knowledge. She supported her nieces and several local women, including Ame and Elizabeth Cuming, in the creation of their own retail shops in Boston. For the next ten years, she would support the well-being of some enterprising young women.

After almost ten years of marriage, on August 4, 1769, James Smith died at their estate. At eighty-one years old, Smith survived much longer than anyone would have expected, and Elizabeth took his loss hard. She

John Singleton Copley painted this portrait of Elizabeth Murray sometime in 1769, shortly after the death of her husband, James Smith. *From the Collection of the Museum of Fine Arts, Boston.*

decided to leave Boston to forget her cares, concentrate on her health and reconnect with friends in Scotland. Seeing her off at the docks on Boston Harbor were her friends and colleagues—and her future husband.

Elizabeth would spend the early part of the 1770s walking a tight line between the two political mindsets of the Patriots and the Loyalists. Try as she might to stay out of the fray, she'd be accused of being a Loyalist by the Sons of Liberty and a Patriot by the Loyalists. But not before she married yet again.

Stand and Defend

Although Elizabeth left Boston, in part, to regain her health, when she arrived back in Boston, life got all the more stressful. Part of that stress was caused by her third husband. Very shortly after her arrival back in Boston, she married another wealthy merchant she'd known for a very long time. Ralph Inman and Elizabeth joined their families and finances on September 26, 1771. Inman agreed to sign a prenuptial agreement that protected the wealth and property left to Elizabeth in her last marriage. Inman also got a little something from the deal—an income from managing her estate. Together, they moved to his farm and property in Cambridge, Massachusetts. (Inman Square, a neighborhood of Cambridge, is believed to be named after Ralph.)

Perhaps in a move that was tone-deaf to the political tension in the air at the time when the colonies moved closer toward breaking ties with Great Britain, Elizabeth had a lavish party at the Cambridge estate to celebrate her stepson's Harvard graduation. By all accounts, it was a fantastic feat—over 250 gentlemen and women attended. But she was roundly criticized in the Boston press. The extravagance of the affair was written about in detail. At the time, austerity in style and manner were praised, as anything smacking of royalty or upper social class was rejected. Elizabeth would be remembered for this.

By the spring of 1775, the Revolution was in full tilt. Elizabeth's family's safety was at risk in Cambridge because the town was perilously close to the action of April 18. Elizabeth did the only thing she could do—she turned her attention to managing her estate and farm to the best of her abilities. While many in the area fled, particularly the women, Elizabeth held on. Her biographer, Patricia Cleary, points out that even Elizabeth's contemporaries found the choice to defend her homestead "marvelous," and Elizabeth herself was aware of that. But for her, it was an easy choice since her family and household depended on her for their safety. Where would they go otherwise? But what of her husband? Good old Ralph was in Boston during the siege. He wasn't trapped behind enemy lines. He stayed there, of his own accord, willfully leaving Elizabeth on her own.

Ralph and Elizabeth's brother James, who had come to Boston after his businesses started to fail in North Carolina, were both Loyalists. This meant that Elizabeth, by association, was considered to be a Loyalist, too. How would this play out, with Elizabeth on her own in the Cambridge countryside? Was she in danger?

She and others like her were in very vulnerable positions both because of their political associations and because they were unprotected women. Her friend Christian Barnes was left to fend for herself in Marlborough, farther to the west of Boston. Elizabeth's husband was now being held against his will in Boston after the colonists turned the tables on the British and surrounded the town. Despite trying to get a letter of protection for herself from the colonial general Israel Putnam, she found herself harassed and in danger. One day, a man showed up on her doorstep and held her at gunpoint, demanding to be fed and for a horse to ride.

If this frightened Elizabeth, she didn't show it. As spring turned to summer, she managed the farm and tried to proceed as normally as possible. This was increasingly difficult to do as rebel soldiers ran rampant over the area. At one point, they held her prisoner in her own home. Word had reached them from one of Inman's slaves that Elizabeth was a traitorous Loyalist. She was able to convince the soldiers otherwise, giving them her word that she would stay in Cambridge and not try to make a break for it. But what could happen next? This prompted her to ask for the assistance of Israel Putnam, whom she knew socially, and he saw fit to station guards on her property. He also assigned his son, Daniel, to stay nights with her to ensure her safety. Daniel Putnam would guide Elizabeth through a midnight ride less celebrated, but no less dramatic, than that of Paul Revere.

On June 17, 1775, General Putnam ordered his son to stay with Elizabeth in Cambridge and not to leave. Something was definitely afoot. They'd heard explosive exchanges all day as British troops captured Bunker Hill. The prevailing thought was that the next move by the British might be to capture the rebel headquarters in Cambridge. It was time to move. That evening, Elizabeth packed up, and she and her family, under Daniel Putnam's guidance, made their way to Brush Hill. The roads were filled with confused travelers; people were anxious for news. They'd met some men who participated in the battle and reported whatever they could. It was a great relief to them both to hear that General Putnam had survived. Daniel traveled back to his father once he delivered Elizabeth safely to Milton. Her vacated Cambridge home was immediately taken over by rebel troops and made Putnam's headquarters. Her farm became a barracks. The estate was left in ruins.

Closing

After the war was over, she and Inman reconciled, but Elizabeth considered moving back to England. Her brother had been banished from Massachusetts for his Loyalist leanings and had died a few years later, leaving her bereft. She missed her friends and felt rootless in the city she'd loved. Before she could leave, she fell ill and decided to take one last look at her will. Despite the ravages of war, she was still a rich woman. She took great care to provide for the young women in her life, friends on both continents, and gave special gifts to her nieces, including her church pew and tomb at King's Chapel in Boston.

She left very little to her husband.

Elizabeth Murray Campbell Smith Inman died on May 25, 1785. She is buried in the family tomb in King's Chapel Burying Ground in downtown Boston.

Chapter 5
STRIDENT SISTERS

Ame and Elizabeth Cuming

Things started out well enough when the two sisters decided to have a go at setting up shop in Boston. They were enjoying the fruits of their labor. They weren't rich by any definition, but they'd been able to support themselves independent of husbands or any male financial support in their lives. When they looked around their shop filled with hats, gloves, bows and ribbons, which some might call trifling things, the sisters were filled with pride. It took a sharp mind to manage and run a retail business. They needed to keep inventory, collect debts, oversee employees, keep up on the latest trends and understand exchange rates, all the while keeping and tending to home, the usual province of women. The life they'd built for themselves was good, and they wouldn't abandon it without a fight.

The political situation was worsening every day. They'd ridden out the tumultuous days after the passage of the Stamp Act in 1765, but the new Townshend Acts were far more onerous. Because the sisters refused to stop selling British goods, the political was getting personal. They were being called enemies of the country in the local papers! Those who didn't comply with the boycott were being treated in ways unimaginable to the two. What they'd seen and heard was shocking, as well as very troubling. Would they be next?

Setting Up Shop

Ame and Elizabeth Cuming were orphaned as young women in Concord, Massachusetts. As women, there were very few options open to them to create their own financial security. Rather than stay on the farm and wait to marry, they decided to take a huge chance and open a shop on their own in the waterfront capital of Boston. Undeterred by their lack of business training and contacts, they enlisted the help of a most unusual mentor—another woman named Elizabeth Murray. A remarkably successful entrepreneur, Elizabeth Murray helped to teach Ame, Elizabeth and many other women in Boston how to become self-sufficient shop owners. With the financial backing of Murray, Ame and Elizabeth started to sell hats for men and women. They eventually expanded their offerings to gloves, handkerchiefs, fabrics and accessories. In an effort to diversify, they expanded their business in 1768 by taking over a small school to teach young women how to embroider.

Most of what they offered in their shop was not manufactured in New England or any of the other colonies in North America. Their inventory of luxury items was strictly from Great Britain. And therein lies the rub. The passage of the Townshend Acts in 1767 made it more difficult, and even dangerous, for the sisters to do business.

Birth, Death and Taxes

When the Stamp Act was passed in 1765, widespread protests broke out up and down the colonies, most of which were orchestrated in Boston. The systematic harassment of customs officials and organized "riots" designed to destroy the property and will of those in favor of the new British taxes ensured that Britain rescinded the tax almost before a cent was collected.

When the Townshend Acts were passed two years later, their message was a strong one from England: Britain could and would tax the colonies; Britain would enforce the collection of taxes by cracking down hard on smuggling; and Britain would use the receipts of those taxes not to protect the colonies but to pay the salaries of colonial governors and judges. The acts also re-affirmed the Writs of Assistance, a general, warrantless search and seizure of suspected smuggled goods. Here was not one, but four, slaps in the face of the colonies. This hardly went over well. Leaders of the resistance to the taxes knew that they would need to fight again to assert their belief in the colonies' need for self-determination, if not full-out independence.

Rejection of the Townshend Acts was swift. Each of the colonies sent a petition to England protesting the tax. While the legislatures pushed this civil tactic of resistance, others were thinking more broadly in terms of protest. A

An image depicting the horrible act of tarring and feathering at the Liberty Tree in Boston. Ame and Elizabeth Cuming witnessed a similar act from the window of their shop. *Library of Congress Prints and Photographs Division Online Catalogue.*

call to boycott all British goods was led by Samuel Adams and John Hancock. Leaders of the opposition, eventually earning the name the Sons of Liberty, asked, and then eventually demanded, that all merchants refuse to import their wares from England. This would be a great sacrifice for those business owners like the Cuming sisters who relied on imported goods to sell, but it would be impossible to keep their doors open otherwise. Some businesses, like grocers or even hardware stores, could buy and resell their goods locally. Wheat could be bought from Pennsylvania and resold in Boston. Nails could be made by the local blacksmith. Fine linens and silks needed to be ordered from England. The Cuming sisters' business was at risk.

The protests of the Townshend Acts also put Loyalists in a compromising position. Loyalists were those business owners who, for political reasons, did not want to make an issue of the tax. They thought that the taxes were a fair price to pay to be a colony of Great Britain. In other words, pay the taxes, keep the peace and move on. They also may not have agreed with the often violent tactics of the Sons of Liberty. Those strategies may have worked to bring about the removal of the Stamp Act, but they had been cruel and at times savage. They would be again. These Loyalists, some of whom were more outspoken than others, were punished severely for their beliefs and actions.

Before long, bands of men representing the Sons of Liberty pressured merchants to formally sign a declaration promising not to import goods. Those who didn't sign immediately were harassed in the most vicious ways. Men were driven out of their shops or homes, beaten in the streets and, in several worst-case scenarios, tarred and feathered. Tar and feathering wasn't just a simple scare tactic. The act involved beating and stripping a man of his clothes and then pouring pine tar over his already bruised body. The man would then be rolled in feathers that would stick to the tar and then paraded about town. The tar would often come off with a layer of skin, leaving the victim bruised and bloody. Occasionally, a lighter version called giving a person a "coat of feathers" would be used as an early warning of sorts. In that case, tar would be applied over the clothes, but the intent and public humiliation was the same.

HARD CHOICES

Regardless of the political feelings of the Cuming sisters, they thought that their little shop was beyond the reach of the mobs and their acts of terror. They believed that they sold only what could be called trifling things. How could these angry men care at all about the bows and ribbons that filled their store? The sisters weren't "fat cats," flouting their riches. They'd played by the rules and ran an honest business. They continued to sell their imported goods. And they wouldn't agree to anything otherwise.

But it was increasingly hard not to have second thoughts. The names of the merchants who wouldn't comply with the boycott were being printed in the Boston newspapers. Worse yet, the address of their place of business was printed alongside their names, so they were that much easier to find. This led to personal violence, as merchants were chased out of their shops and beaten in the streets. It also led to one of the most tragic events in the run-up to the Revolutionary War—the killing of a young boy named Christopher Seider.

On February 22, 1770, a crowd of boys was hanging around outside the shop of a known Loyalist, Theophilius Lillie. The gang harassed Lillie, throwing stones, snowballs and ice at his shop and his customers. They went so far as to hang him in effigy from his own storefront. There was no mistaking the identity of the effigy—it held a sign screaming "Importer!" Lillie's good friend and fellow Loyalist Ebenezer Richardson rushed to the store to give Lillie a hand at dispersing the crowd. Instead, Richardson's arrival aroused the crowd even more, and they chased him back to his North End home. As snow, ice and rocks came crashing into his home, he became furious. He brandished a gun, pointing it at the growing crowd and threatening to pull the trigger unless they dispersed. They didn't. Instead, his actions had emboldened the crowd. Richardson soon lost control and fired. When the smoke of the gunfire lifted, it revealed a small boy lying on the ground with a bloody gut. Poor Christopher Seider would not live through the night. As news of his death spread through the town, another mob arrived at Richardson's door. This time, their intention wasn't just to harass but to deliver revenge. If it weren't for some cool heads prevailing, another death might have occurred that day.

This was the tense environment in which Ame and Elizabeth were living and doing business. Still, they wouldn't comply with the boycott. At first, they even got some business out of it from others who thought the mobs were going too far. In fact, they told their friend Elizabeth Murray that they'd actually ended the year with "mor custom then before." This would not last.

When a shipment of English goods arrived, they could have stored it in a warehouse for safekeeping and not unloaded it into their store for sale. But onto the shelves it all went. Before long, a group of men arrived, accusing the sisters of not acting in accordance with the boycott. They told the men

A LIST of the Names of *those* who AUDACIOUSLY continue to counteract the UNITED SENTIMENTS of the BODY of Merchants thro'out NORTH-AMERICA; by importing British Goods contrary to the Agreement.

John Bernard,
    (In King-Street, almost opposite Vernon's Head.

James McMasters,
        (On Treat's Wharf.

Patrick McMasters,
    (Opposite the Sign of the Lamb.

John Mein,
    (Opposite the White-Horse, and in King-Street.

Ame & Elizabeth Cummings,
(Opposite the Old Brick Meeting House, all of Boston.

And, *Henry Barnes,*
    (Trader in the Town of Marlboro'.

HAVE, and do still continue to import Goods from London, contrary to the Agreement of the Merchants.—They have been requested to Store their Goods upon the same Terms as the rest of the Importers have done, but absolutely refuse, by conducting in this Manner.

IT must evidently appear that they have prefered their own little private Advantage to the Welfare of America : It is therefore highly proper that the Public should know who they are, that have at this critical Time, sordidly detached themselves from the public Interest ; and as they will be deemed Enemies to their Country, by all who are well-wishers to it ; so those who afford them their Countenance or give them their Custom, must expect to be considered in the same disagreeable Light.

Ame and Elizabeth Cuming are named among those "audaciously" flouting the agreement against importing British goods. Their shop's address is also noted. The listing ran in the *Boston Gazette* on January 22, 1770. *Courtesy of the American Antiquarian Society.*

that they'd never signed anything to that effect and would continue business as usual. Their names and the address of their shop were made public a short time later. Would they or their business be the next to suffer abuse? They were.

On October 28, 1769, Elizabeth was visiting a sick friend when she heard a terrible screaming. It was their friend John Mein, the publisher of the only Loyalist newspaper in Boston, racing up the street followed by an unlikely mob—a mob who wore gentlemen's clothing. Elizabeth was shocked to see some of Boston's most upstanding individuals chasing Mein, wielding their canes like swords, out for blood. Mein managed to escape with his life, but the mob wasn't finished. Instead, that night they went hunting for another Loyalist, a customs official turned informer named George Gailer. Gailer was caught, beaten to a bloody "gore" and then thrown onto a cart. But the mob's violence didn't stop there. They delivered Gailer to the doorstep of Ame and Elizabeth as the sisters cowered inside. Then, the mob, making a very fine point to the sisters, tarred and feathered Gailer's bloody body. Writhing in pain and made to hold a lantern aloft, Gailer was carried through the streets of Boston while the mob admonished all to put candles in their windows to support their savage work.

Even after that horribly graphic demonstration, the sisters pressed on, with seeming bravado. But as the violence increased with the killing of Christopher Seider and the Boston Massacre, the killing of five colonists by British regulars days later on March 5, 1770, the sisters weren't able to resist the boycott for much longer. Finally, it was the printing of the names of their customers in the newspapers that proved to be the last straw. Any support they still had disappeared. Their days as business owners in Boston were over.

Bon Voyage

The sisters relocated to their birthplace of Concord, Massachusetts, and rode out the years between the massacre and the start of the Revolutionary War there. When ships of Loyalists started to leave Boston for Nova Scotia, they were on board. They settled in Halifax, set up shop and started all over again. Although they missed their friends, they'd landed on their feet and "were more prosperous than ever they were in Boston."

Chapter 6
THE MISTRESS AND THE SULTANA

Dorcas Griffiths and Elizabeth Lloyd Loring

*I*n times of love and war, sometimes picking the right partner isn't exactly clear. These two women chose to align with the wrong side, at least in war. For one woman, things worked out well. For the other, life was much harder.

The story of the Loyalists is not well told in our Revolutionary War history. The focus is always on the heroes of battle, the daring forays into enemy territory, the David-and-Goliath drama of a small band of rebels taking on the largest military force in the world and coming away the victor. The story of those who sided with the Crown gets lost—partly because history is written by the victors and partly because the losers were treated so badly by those same heroes and rebels. It's a history some might prefer to forget.

Just as in the Civil War, families and friends were torn apart based on loyalties and ideologies. One of those was Lucy Flucker Knox, the wife of Henry Knox, the Patriot bookseller who became the first United States secretary of war. She was disowned by her family, who were rabid Loyalists. Her brother fought for the British army, and her family left with the British evacuation of Boston in March 1776, leaving Lucy alone and her husband off at war.

The Fluckers weren't the only Loyalists who left at that turbulent time, leaving behind whatever they couldn't carry—their property, their homes, their friends and family. Most traveled to Halifax, Nova Scotia, and either settled in the Canadian Maritimes or went on to England.

One who left for England by way of Halifax to make a go at a new life was Dorcas Pringle Griffiths. While in Boston, she was the mistress of none other than John Hancock, outsized signer of the Declaration of Independence, a key Patriot leader and one of the wealthiest men in all of Boston.

Elizabeth Lloyd Loring also eventually wound up in England but only after a decadent detour. She was the wife of Joshua Loring Jr., but she traveled openly in the company of General William Howe. This caused a firestorm of criticism for the general, but her husband reaped the benefits of essentially renting out his wife. In her dual roles as wife and mistress, she was popularly known as the "Sultana."

THE MISTRESS

Dorcas Pringle Griffiths was born in Boston on August 31, 1720; was married to Thomas Griffiths in 1742; and had a daughter, Sarah. Dorcas and Thomas ran a shop together out of their home at the head of Hancock's Wharf selling groceries, tea and linens, eventually obtaining a license to sell liquor. After her husband died, Dorcas was rumored to have expanded the business to include the world's oldest profession. The merchants, sailors and seafarers she met on the wharf would have made for a steady market. Her most famous paramour, though, was John Hancock, who may have delayed marriage to socially prominent Dorothy Quincy because of his affair with the much less socially prominent (and acceptable) Dorcas.

Dorothy pursued Hancock for years, and no one understood why he was dragging his feet. Dorcas, something of a cougar at eighteen years Hancock's senior, appeared to have a hold on him. It was rumored that he subsidized her living arrangements so that she lived a little more comfortably than the ordinary shopkeeper—until the Battle of Bunker Hill, that is, when their opposing viewpoints clashed. Dorcas was loyal to the Crown, and Hancock was the popular leader of the Sons of Liberty. The differences were irreconcilable. Two months after Bunker Hill, Dorothy Quincy and John Hancock were married.

That meant Dorcas was on her own financially, and during the British Siege of Boston, she stayed in town and tended to the needs of British officers and soldiers. She nursed one marine, David Johnston, back to health after the Battle of Bunker Hill and got friendly with some of the officers, like Generals Gage and Howe. She and her daughter left

Boston on Evacuation Day, heading for Halifax and eventually arriving in London in December 1778.

Americans like Dorcas, who supported the Crown in the war, could seek payment from the British government for the damages they suffered. One fantastic story is of John Malcolm, who was tarred and feathered for his rather obnoxious and outspoken support of the King in the days prior to the Revolution. He personally presented charred chunks of his own skin to the King and pledged his ever-lasting honor.

Dorcas didn't have to go quite that far. She needed only to submit a petition asking for a pension by giving an accounting of the value of her lost possessions, backed up with letters endorsing her word and character. Dorcas brought out the big guns, as such men as General Gage, General William Howe (who will resurface later in this story) and Lord Percy all wrote letters in her support. For this, she and her daughter received a small pension from July 5, 1779, until it abruptly stopped in 1782. But why did it stop?

Enter Thomas Flucker, the father of Lucy Knox. Prior to fleeing Boston on Evacuation Day, he was the last secretary of the province of Massachusetts. In London, Flucker was appointed to the Loyalist Compensation Commission and used his power to pass judgment on Dorcas in, for her, a most unfortunate way. Despite the recognition of several of Britain's leading lights backing her loyalty and honor, Flucker remembered what he'd heard about her relationship with a leading Revolutionary, as well as less savory details about her private life in Boston. His official report states that Dorcas "was a Common prostitute and bred up her Daughter in the same way." Her name was ruined, and despite another petition with additional recommendations from merchants supporting the legitimacy of, at least, her grocery business, it would be in vain. Dorcas would receive nothing further for her support of the Crown and whatever assistance she had offered to British soldiers in Boston. She lived out the rest of her days in poverty.

THE SULTANA

Things worked out rather differently for Elizabeth Lloyd Loring. Born of the upper classes in Dorchester, now a neighborhood of Boston, and married to prominent Loyalist Joshua Loring Jr., her social class would make her experience as a refugee much different than that of Dorcas. Just as Dorcas is assumed to have done, Elizabeth used her sexuality to her advantage, but with very different results.

Elizabeth, known as a blue-eyed beauty, caught the eye of General William Howe—the very same William Howe who stood up for Dorcas during her petition for a pension in England—during the Siege of Boston. The two became a notorious item, and it appears they did nothing to hide their affair.

Elizabeth evacuated to Halifax, but instead of relocating to London, she went to New York City to be by the general's side, with her husband in tow. Joshua Loring managed to get something out of the deal; he turned a blind eye to his wife's affair when he was given the position of commissary of prisoners for the British army. The commissary was set up to take care of prisoners of war, but he decided the funds would be better used for his own enrichment. His embezzlement likely caused the deaths of at least three hundred American soldiers by leaving them to starve.

Meanwhile, Elizabeth's affair with the general was so public that poetry was written about them:

> *Sir William, he, snug as a flea,*
> *Lay all the time a-snoring;*
> *Nor dreamed of harm, as he lay warm*
> *In bed with Mrs. L____g.*

Loyalists, as well as General Howe's fellow officers, became deeply concerned about the affair. To them, it seemed that Elizabeth was all the general cared to think about. They wined, dined and gambled together. He was supposed to be leading the army to victory in what was generally agreed to be an easy war to win; instead, he sat on his hands and lost opportunities to pursue the rebels. General Howe was a lifelong professional soldier, and his officers were enraged to think that he was allowing a woman to cloud his thinking. Together, the couple enjoyed a war-time social season in New York.

Such a firm grip on the general earned Elizabeth the nickname, among others, of the "Sultana," a more romantic and tasteful word for a sultan's concubine. A New York Loyalist, Judge Thomas Jones, especially galled by the behavior of the general, called her "the General's Cleopatra" after that other bombshell who spoiled the military career of Marc Anthony.

When General Howe resigned his duties in 1778, Elizabeth returned to her husband, who continued to run the commissary. She left the former colonies with her children later that same year. Loring would eventually join them, and in the absence of General Howe, she and her husband had

This German woodcut shows the British evacuation of Boston, Massachusetts, on March 17, 1776. *Library of Congress Prints and Photographs Division Online Catalogue.*

three more children. Loring died in 1789, prompting Elizabeth to petition the same governmental panel as Dorcas for relief for Loyalist Americans. Writing on behalf of Elizabeth's character was none other than her former paramour General William Howe. Elizabeth was granted a pension, which she collected until her death in 1830.

It paid to have social standing and connections, which Dorcas didn't. Dorcas chose to sleep with the enemy before making her eventual allegiance with the British. Whatever help she may have provided them didn't measure up when word got around that she was a prostitute—or that she'd had an affair with Hancock. Loring had the best of both worlds—she lived in the lap of luxury before, during and after the war.

Chapter 7
SIREN SONG

Rachel Wall

She thought hard about what she was going to write. Her life had been filled with ups and downs, and now, after only twenty-nine years, she was coming to the end of it. Would she do it over again? She smiled to herself as she reminisced about her adventures on the high seas north of Boston. Her crimes were too numerous to mention. It wasn't pretty sometimes, but she and her husband had pulled off a few major capers. Thinking of her husband, she realized how much she missed him. She'd soon join him in whatever version of an afterlife one cared to believe in, if one cared to believe—maybe Heaven, maybe Hell. Either way, she'd be dead soon—and for a crime she didn't even commit! How's that for irony? She'd gotten away with so much, and so much worse, that to be hanged for highway robbery—well, it was almost insulting. So while she had the chance, she would write her life's story, and it would be published as a broadside for all to read and wonder at in Boston in 1789.

WHERE IT ALL BEGAN

Rachel Wall was born in Carlisle, Pennsylvania, in 1760. Her parents were hardworking, pious farmers who were none too taken with her choice of husband, George Wall. George was a sailor who swept Rachel off her feet— and back to Boston with him. Rachel's parents' assessment of George was spot-on. George was a ne'er-do-well who often ran into trouble with the law. Once, while George was in the clink, Rachel baked him a tool-laden cake in an effort to break him out, proving that the two were made for each other. Unfortunately, when he wasn't incarcerated, George didn't stick around for long, going to sea for long stretches at a time. Rachel became a servant during his absences, but upon his latest return, he'd hit upon another far more lucrative, but far less legal, plan. He asked Rachel to join him and a few cronies on a seafaring adventure, one that would make them rich. George schemed and persuaded a friend to give his band of merry mates a fast fishing schooner in return for a share of their catch. But it wasn't fishing George had in mind—unless it was fishing for unwitting dupes.

The Pirate's Life

Rachel and George's crew set out, but at the first sign of stormy weather, they put in to harbor at the Isles of Shoals off the coast of New Hampshire and Maine to ride out the conditions. With the return of clearing weather, they sailed away into the midst of the heavily trafficked shipping lanes

A postcard of the ledge on the Isles of Shoals in New Hampshire. It looks like a perfectly suitable hiding place for a band of pirates. *Courtesy of the Trustees of the Boston Public Library.*

around the New England coast. Once there, they took down their sails and put up a distress signal. Once a ship was within sight, Rachel got to work hailing them, begging for assistance. Since a crying, helpless woman was too hard for many sailors to resist, the ploy worked. Once a ship came to help, its crew was welcomed aboard—and knifed to death. The pirate crew took everything of value off the rescuing ship and sunk it, along with the weighted bodies of the dead. Then, they sold off everything that they claimed to have found washed ashore on the Isles of Shoals in the wake of the storm.

Rachel and her husband's successful game lasted for at least a year, bringing the two and their accomplices a tidy and consistent income. When they ran out of cash, all they had to do was wait out another storm and feast on the kindness of strangers. Until, that is, George got over-confident. Back off the Isles of Shoals, one storm wasn't quite over when they left their safe harbor to attract the next unsuspecting crew—it was, in fact, the eye of the storm. Too late to turn back, the fury of the storm tore the ship apart, tossing George and another crew member to their deaths in the high, raging waves. A brig from New York picked up the surviving crew and delivered a grieving Rachel back to Boston. She decided that the pirate's life just wasn't for her anymore.

THE LIFE OF THE HIGHWAYWOMAN

Rachel went back to work as a servant, but the life of crime and adventure was too hard to resist. And one always needed a little extra cash. So she put her knowledge of ships and sailors to work. At night, Rachel would sneak aboard the ships anchored at the Long Wharf in Boston Harbor while their captains were asleep or carousing in town. She took whatever caught her fancy. She knew that most captains kept their most valuable items hidden in the "head" or toilet, and that's where she found the best booty—gold coins, silver watches— all for the taking. She was wildly successful. But all good things must come to an end. She was caught red-handed and dragged into court to defend herself in 1785. She pleaded guilty and was ordered to pay damages and court costs and be lashed fifteen times across her naked back. She had no money to pay, so she was indentured for three years to pay off her debt.

Three years to the day later, it was déjà vu all over again. She was back in court, pleading guilty to housebreaking and theft. Again, she was ordered to pay court costs and damages, as well as sit for an hour on the gallows with a noose around her neck. Again, it was impossible for her to pay her debt, and again, she was indentured for three years.

A BIG MISUNDERSTANDING

Gainfully employed and supposedly avoiding a life of crime, Rachel was mixed up in the theft of the bonnet of a well-to-do young woman named Margaret Bender. On the evening of March 27, 1789, the seventeen-year-old Margaret was walking home when a woman emerged from the darkness and attempted to steal the bonnet right off Margaret's head. Margaret was thrown to the ground. The thief didn't stop with her bonnet but ripped off her shoes and buckles and ran off into the night. Margaret's mouth was bloodied, and she was obviously shaken. Two men came to her aid; one sat with her as the other took off after the crook. He returned with a protesting Rachel Wall. Margaret confirmed Rachel as the perpetrator, and Rachel's fate was sealed.

Although Rachel protested her innocence, her past was just too corrupt, and the evidence was too strong against her. She was ordered executed for highway robbery and was hanged on Boston Common on October 10, 1789. She was the last woman hanged in Massachusetts.

Chapter 8
NINETEEN AND PREGNANT

Mary Patten

*A*s crowds swelled on the dock below Mary Patten, she watched people gather in the July heat to see off the ship *Neptune's Car* and its bold and handsome captain, her husband, Joshua. They were out to prove that *Neptune's Car* was the fastest clipper ship in America in 1856, and Mary was pleased to see so many had turned out.

A new age of shipping and seafaring began in the late 1840s with the introduction of the clipper ship. Much faster than their predecessors, clipper ships were developed to meet the demand for fast and efficient shipping across the world. The gold rush in 1849 opened up California to new settlers looking to strike it rich. Merchants followed along to open new markets in the burgeoning port of San Francisco, and demand for fast shipping and travel grew. Prior to the introduction of the clipper ship, there were primarily two ways to get to California from the East Coast: over the California Trail, which was a treacherous overland journey filled with dangerous weather, dangerous terrain and dangerous natives; or by the so-called sea route, which involved taking a ship to Panama, going overland by train or wagon and then taking another ship up the coast to Sacramento. The greatest danger on this route was avoiding infection by a tropical disease while traveling through the jungles of Panama. Otherwise, it was a cake walk. Neither route was particularly pleasant or expeditious, but ninety thousand people made their way to California in 1849 alone. There was one less popular way to get there: a captain feeling particularly lucky could take a ship from the East Coast all the way down the coast of South America, around the tip of Cape Horn and

The American clipper ship *Challenge* of New York. *Challenge* is a typical clipper ship, very similar in style and size to the *Neptune's Car*. This image was published by N. Currier between 1835 and 1856. *Library of Congress Prints and Photographs Online Catalogue.*

then back up to the West Coast of the United States. This voyage, if it could be completed at all, could take as long as eight months—until the clipper ships arrived on the scene. This is what they were built for. Clipper ships cut the travel time from New York City to San Francisco to four months.

The excitement around this way of traveling culminated in a competition among three ships to see which could make the journey in under one hundred days. An almost impossible record had been set by Captain Josiah Cressy in 1851; he took the *Flying Cloud* from New York to San Francisco in just eighty-nine days.

The smart money was on Captain Patten, who had already made the trip in just under 101 days, and the crew of the *Neptune's Car* to beat the *Romance of the Seas* and the *Intrepid*. But by the time *Neptune's Car* arrived in San Francisco on November 15, 1856, a different Captain Patten would be at the helm—and she would be four months pregnant.

Stormy Weather

The journey started out well enough as the new crew settled in and got to work. Because Captain Patten's first mate broke his leg just before the trip, a substitute, a Mr. Keeler, was found. Within a few days, it was clear that Keeler was either not up to the task of performing his duties or was being paid off by one of the *Neptune's Car*'s competitors to tank their chances of winning the race. No amount of threats or reprimands would move Keeler. The situation became untenable—not only money but also pride was at stake here. Keeler was ordered locked up in the brig.

Unfortunately, that left the captain to take on double duties. His second mate, Mr. Hare, was a skilled sailor but illiterate and unable to navigate the ship. Being short-handed could not have come at a worse time; the southern hemisphere was still in the grips of what turned out to be one of the worst winters on record. *Neptune's Car* ran into stormy weather—fifty-foot waves, gale-force winds and freezing temperatures. For eight days and nights, Captain Patten guided his ship through the fierce conditions, refusing to leave the deck. As he tried to out-run the cold, wind and waves, exhaustion and sickness caught up to him. Captain Patten fell so severely ill with what was then called "brain fever" that he had bouts of deafness and blindness. Taking care of him was his wife, Mary, who soon realized that the fate of the *Neptune's Car* and its crew was squarely on her shoulders. First Mate Keeler was in lockup. Second Mate Hare simply couldn't get the job done. Mary had to take over.

Hard Decisions

Mary Patten was born in East Boston on April 6, 1837, and married Joshua at the age of sixteen at the Old North Church—the very same church whose steeple hoisted two lanterns signaling that the redcoats were on the move to Concord and Lexington by sea. Every time Mary's husband went to sea, she didn't sit idly by on a mythical widow's watch waiting for her man to reappear. She, and other women like her, accompanied her husband. This was normally a somewhat boring proposition because there was very little for a woman to do on board a ship. Mary did contribute by cooking and nursing sick sailors, and in quiet moments, she asked her husband to teach her how to read the chronometer and sextant and use the telescope. She learned the art of navigating by the stars and position of the sun, and she knew how to chart a

The Old North Church as seen from Hull Street in 1898. Mary Brown married Captain Joshua Adam Patten here in 1853. *Courtesy of the Trustees of the Boston Public Library.*

course. Her husband commented that, if it was possible (and it wasn't at the time), Mary could certainly have become a master mariner.

And it was a good thing, too—these were the talents and skills the crew was lacking with their captain incapacitated and their first mate jailed. Mary gathered the crew together and told them that she was taking over.

When First Mate Keeler was tipped off about the change in leadership, he wrote a letter to Mary arguing that he should be reinstated. But Mary knew

"Docks, East Boston." A drawing by Maurice Brazil Prendergast shows the busy port near where Mary Patten grew up. *Collection of Mr. and Mrs. Paul Mellon, in Honor of the 50th Anniversary of the National Gallery of Art—1992. Courtesy of the National Gallery of Art.*

that there was no way she could trust him, given his previous behavior, and told him so. Hell hath no fury like a first mate scorned—Keeler tried his best to incite mutiny in the crew to overthrow Mary. No one took the bait.

It's hard to fathom how a nineteen-year-old woman could compel a ship full of hardscrabble sailors to stand behind her, but they did. Although together they endured the fury of the sea, harder times were still ahead. Mary had to make a tough decision to go off course in an effort to find calmer waters—a direction that would put them dangerously close to Antarctica, more freezing temperatures and the constant threat of icebergs. After careful navigation through an ice field, the ship finally came around Cape Horn.

All this time, Mary not only commanded the ship but also continued to nurse her sick husband. Who says you can't have it all?

As the ship approached the equator, Captain Patten had a sudden recovery. In an attempt to give his wife and Mr. Hare a break, he asked Keeler to return to his original duties. Good deeds never go unpunished; Keeler was found to be taking the ship not to its ultimate destination but to Chile instead! Mary suspected that this was the case, and after Captain Patten had a compass built in his quarters to keep tabs on the situation, he found that she was correct and jailed Keeler for good.

Captain Patten's recovery was short-lived, however, and Mary took command for the next month, finally reaching San Francisco on November 15, 1856. The journey took 136 days, and Mary was acting captain for more than 50 of those days. While the *Romance of the Seas* had arrived a few days prior, the *Neptune's Car* still beat the *Intrepid*, whose captain was wildly (and rightly) impressed with Mary's fortitude, leadership and sailing skills.

The next trip the Pattens needed to make was back home to Boston, where they arrived in February 1857. Two and a half weeks later, a healthy Joshua Adam Patten Jr. had made his own little successful journey into the world. Sadly, just a few months later, in July, Captain Patten succumbed to tuberculosis. In his honor, flags were flown at half mast over Boston Harbor.

A group of insurers were so impressed by Mary that they rewarded her with a check for $1,000 for the safe arrival of their cargo on the *Neptune's Car*. She demurely accepted but typically claimed that it was not she who deserved the credit but First Mate Hare and the supportive crew of the *Neptune's Car*. After her husband's death, more support arrived from donations made by the ladies of Boston society.

Mary had no interest in the fame that came along with her impossible passage. She spent the too-short remainder of her life raising her son with her mother in the North End, a rough neighborhood filled with seafarers and merchants. She died in 1861, also of tuberculosis. She is buried by her husband's side in Woodlawn Cemetery in Everett, Massachusetts, with a nondescript but serviceable gravestone—just as Mary would have liked.

Portrait of Mary Ann Brown Patten (navigator and sailor, 1837–1861). Ninth-plate ambrotype. Gift of Dorthy Knouse Koepke, S/NPG.2006.55, National Portrait Gallery, Smithsonian Institution, Washington, D.C., USA. *National Portrait Gallery, Smithsonian Institution/ Art Resource, New York.*

Chapter 9
PROTO–ROSA PARKS

Sarah Parker Remond

On December 1, 1955, Rosa Parks refused to obey the demand of a bus driver to move from her seat designated for whites only in Montgomery, Alabama. Her act and the resultant protests that she inspired became a beacon for the civil rights movement of the 1950s and '60s. She became internationally known as the standard-bearer of an entire movement, eventually receiving the Presidential Medal of Freedom and the Congressional Gold Medal. She's honored with a statue in the National Statuary Hall at the United States Capitol Building and, on her death, was the first woman to lie in honor at the Capitol Rotunda. Parks very much deserved all these honors. But another woman acted similarly over one hundred years prior, and you probably have never heard of her. Until now.

ACT 1, SCENE 1

The scene was set at Boston's Howard Athenaeum in the spring of 1853. A well-heeled woman and her two friends were trying to attend an opera at the theater. Dressed for the evening out and looking forward to the show, the three were making their way to their seats in the "Family Circle" when they were abruptly stopped by the manager. He refused to let them through. The three guests were asked, instead, to take different seats in the upper balcony. The three had paid for better seats in the "Family Circle" and expected

Portrait of Sarah Parker Remond. Photograph. Dimensions: image: 8.5 cm x 5.2 cm; approximate size of mount 22.8 cm x 7.5 cm. From *Portraits of American Abolitionists*. Photo. 81.448. *Collection of the Massachusetts Historical Society.*

to enjoy them. When one of the guests absolutely refused to move, an argument ensued, and the police were called in.

Calling the police seems a little heavy-handed, but the management was white and the three theatergoers were black. Despite being a theater, this was a scene the management couldn't afford. Unfortunately, a scene was just what they got in a real-life drama that would unfold over the subsequent weeks. Sarah Parker Remond had reached her limit with racism in Boston. While Boston may have been more liberal than other cities in the United States in 1853, racism was alive and well. The upper balcony she and her friends were asked to move to was called "nigger heaven" because it was the only area in which people of color were allowed to sit. Sarah believed that policy would need to change.

She would stand her ground. She and her friends were forcibly removed and pushed down the stairs and out the door. Sarah's dress was torn, and her shoulder was hurt in the struggle. She would not tolerate this treatment. She would fight for her rights and demand satisfaction. She would not be refused. This was just the opening salvo of what became a lifelong journey of standing her ground, refusing to settle for less and never being afraid to fight for justice.

The course of Sarah's life might have been different had it not been for the treatment she received at the Howard Athenaeum on that night in 1853. While the theater in Scollay Square would go on to become the notorious "Old Howard," home to burlesque and strip shows in the 1940s, '50s and '60s, and would eventually burn to the ground, Sarah would also become notorious. She went to court and fought for the damages for both her rough treatment and the value of her opera ticket. She won when the judge awarded her more than $500 in damages. She had won a milestone case that upheld "the equal rights of our Colored citizens." She won a name for herself. She won the opportunity to speak to crowds eager to hear the message of a free black woman. She won influence. She did not let those wins or the opportunities and influence go to waste.

Separate but Not Equal

Sarah Parker Remond was born in Salem, Massachusetts, in 1826. She was the daughter of free black parents who were doing well financially for themselves and their family in the catering and hairdressing businesses. Her parents took education very seriously, understanding its importance as a cornerstone of success. Sarah and her seven brothers and sisters were all educated at home. They were lucky enough to have a fair number of books. But Sarah's parents knew it wasn't enough. The children should attend school for better instruction and books.

Salem was a bit ahead of its time with regard to schooling black children, but even that had its limits. In the early 1830s, black children could attend public schools with whites, but that situation did not last long. Sarah and her siblings attended a mixed primary school, but by the time they passed the entrance tests and were accepted to the secondary school, opinions were changing. While the people of Salem were supportive of educating blacks in the community (and would even pay taxes for it!), they did not want that to come, as noted by the local news editorials, "at the expense of their children." In an episode that is all too similar to the battles over segregated schools and busing policies in the 1970s, the Salem School Committee voted to set up a separate school for blacks. Separate, but not equal. The school would keep all black children together in a single room, and they'd be taught together regardless of age or ability. White children had options for both primary and secondary schooling—the difference between grade school and high school today. The Remond family protested this change of policy and left Salem altogether after their demands for equal educational opportunities were not met. They moved to Newport, Rhode Island, where the children attended an all-black private school.

FAMILY AFFAIR

By the 1840s, the Remonds had moved back to Salem and become active in the abolitionist movement. Sarah's brother, Charles Lenox Remond, became a community leader in both Salem and Boston; he started to lecture all over the United States and was, in fact, the American Anti-Slavery Society's first black speaker. Sarah's father was an active member of the Massachusetts Anti-Slavery Society, so it was just a matter of time before Sarah took up the mantle of reformer, as well.

Sarah's family also stayed involved in changing public education policy. In 1844, Salem became the first municipality in Massachusetts to mandate racial integration of its public schools. This led the Remonds to often take in black children so that they might take advantage of Salem's public schools. One such child was Charlotte Forten. Charlotte would become a firebrand herself by becoming not only an active abolitionist but also the first black woman to teach white children in Massachusetts. Charlotte considered Sarah to be a significant mentor.

LIBERALLY SPEAKING

In 1841, Sarah made her first public speech. She was a natural. By 1856, she was traveling across the United States as a speaker. In 1859, at the age of thirty-three, she left the Boston area and began to lecture all over Great Britain. She was such a popular speaker in England that, over the Christmas season in 1859, she lectured at least eight times in six cities in the span of three weeks. And remember, there was no Underground for rapid transit at the time.

It was not common to hear from a woman, let alone a black woman. She was the first black person many had ever seen in England. She spoke from the heart, not as a former slave but as a free woman who had experienced discrimination unlike any of her listeners had ever experienced. She spoke directly to women's fears about the physical and sexual abuse female slaves were subjected to and about their children being torn away from them. In a free and democratic country, this brutality endured. She brought tears to their eyes. This was a fear they could all relate to.

She admitted that her popularity in Britain surprised her. She was notably anxious about making the trip, assuming that she would be met with the ill will she was used to in the United States. This was simply not the case. She said, "I have been received here as a sister of white women for the first time in my life. I have been removed from the degradation which overhangs all persons of my complexion." Sadly, she encountered continued discrimination only from her own country. In 1859, the American Embassy in London refused to grant her a passport to speak in France. Again, she stood up for her rights and won.

She spent the years during the Civil War in Great Britain and Europe, raising money and building support for the Union's blockade of Confederate forces and trade interests. Although her lecture schedule was hectic, with more than forty-five lectures in twenty-five cities and towns in England, Scotland and Ireland in the span of three years, she also managed to continue her studies at the Bedford College for Ladies in London and to travel to Italy. She returned to the United States after the war to support the entry of free blacks into society, raising money for their care. She also became more involved in the rights of women in general. When those efforts were thwarted, she returned to Europe, never to step foot on American soil again.

Never one to slow down, she took up a new cause. At the age of forty-two, she moved permanently to Florence, Italy, and entered medical school. She spent the rest of her days practicing medicine, married to an Italian man. She died in Florence and is interred in Rome's Protestant Cemetery.

Chapter 10

BIKER BABES

Kittie Knox, Annie Kopchovsky and Mary Sargent Hopkins

*I*t was 1895, dubbed the Gilded Age by Mark Twain. Just before the turn of a new century, change was in the air in the United States. Industry was booming. The rich were getting richer. Immigrants were flooding into the cities, which, in turn, were growing by leaps and bounds. Skyscrapers burst from the ground. New railroads connected city to city. Laborers demanded unions. Women demanded the vote. Teetotalers demanded temperance. In the midst of this upheaval, three women played their part to force change in Boston—all while sitting astride their bicycles. One woman would cross the color line. Another would cross into some thirteen countries. And the third did more to popularize cycling for women across the United States than anyone else, all the while clucking her tongue at the two mavericks, criticizing not their accomplishments but their attire.

CRAZED

Bicycles have been around for a long time, but until recently, they were seen mostly as playthings for children. During the past few decades, Americans have become increasingly aware of the issue of sustainability and environmental issues. We've looked for transportation alternatives to the automobile. At the same time, we've also looked for more ways to enjoy the outdoors and encourage exercise. Bicycling has been one answer.

Mary Sargent Hopkins would frown on this type of cycling for ladies. This photo is from a stereoscope photograph published in 1897. *Courtesy of the Trustees of the Boston Public Library.*

The first verifiable design of something akin to what we'd recognize as a bike today was engineered in Germany in the early 1800s. This contraption didn't even have pedals, but over the next sixty years, the design evolved. Turning handlebars were added. Brakes came in handy. Tricycles were introduced and became popular for a time. Eventually, the design was refined to the style we're familiar with today, creating what was called the "safety bicycle." Mass production was perfected by Bostonian Albert Augustus Pope in his Back Bay factory, making the bicycle more affordable. By the 1890s, its popularity exploded, ushering in what is known as the bicycle craze.

Bicycle riding clubs started to pop up all over the United States. Riding tours were being set up in every major American city. The same groups advocated for safer roads for riding. Importantly, bicycle riding didn't just appeal to men; it appealed to women, as well. The bicycle craze opened doors for women in ways they'd never known of before. Cycling offered both spiritual freedom and physical freedom of movement throughout the world. It offered independence. It culminated in power and self-determination. Women found a freedom in bicycle riding that they would not let go to waste.

KITTIE KNOX

The League of American Wheelmen was founded in 1880 as a national umbrella group to organize local clubs proliferating all over the United States. By 1893, the league was facing some challenges that threatened the longevity of the organization. A faction in Louisville, Kentucky, was pushing to disallow African Americans to join. The measure was passed at the league's annual meeting in 1894. It claimed that the inclusion of African Americans was hurting the opportunity for the club to grow in the southern states. The *New York Times* and *Chicago Record* both decried the legislation, as did many league members. The Massachusetts state legislature went so far as to pass a resolution stating its stand against the measure. Local clubs, governed by their own bylaws, still had the ability to allow anyone to join. The Riverside Cycling Club of Cambridge, Massachusetts, was Boston's first all-black cycling club, and it had at least one exceptional member: Kittie Knox. She was about to challenge and embarrass the league at an upcoming meet in New Jersey in 1895.

Kittie was born in Cambridgeport, an African American neighborhood in Cambridge, on October 7, 1874, to a white mother and black father. Her father died when she was seven years old, and she was raised by her mother and older brother in the West End of Boston. In her adulthood, she became a seamstress and an unlikely superstar cyclist.

By the 1890s, Kittie was on the bicycling scene. Both the white and black local press praised her "graceful" performances in local races and meets. More than anything, her looks, or more specifically her color, raised comments. The "beautiful and buxom black bloomerite" was a local hit. Kittie performed at local meets in either races or in a variety of other contests, including a costuming contest that she won at a

A photo of Kittie Knox taken at the Asbury Meet in New Jersey. Kittie is decked out in the bloomers she fashioned for herself. *Courtesy of the Smithsonian Institution.*

Waltham Cycle Park meet in July 1895. How she won the meet is actually astonishing in its way. Not only was she African American, but she was also wearing bloomers, a controversial choice at the time.

It may have been the win that emboldened her or an understanding of the support she had from the Massachusetts delegation, but Kittie decided to attend the league's national annual gathering at Asbury Park, New Jersey, later in July 1895. As historian Lorenz J. Finison explains, this was all the more remarkable because Asbury Park was not a community known to be welcoming to African Americans. Dressed in a striking bloomer costume, Kittie rode her bicycle in front of the very exclusive Asbury Park clubhouse, strode inside and presented her membership card. She was initially turned away due to her color.

She must have known that she would be rejected, and she seemed to take it all in stride. Her argument for attending was that she was a card-carrying member of the league—before it passed the color restriction. Some were pushing an argument that the ban on African Americans was only for applicants to the league and not to members in good standing. To all appearances, Kittie tested that argument, and she eventually won.

Her act of defiance was covered in the national news, and she was ultimately allowed to participate in the event when a high-standing member of another club spoke to officials on her behalf. She made her point, and she made it well—she took part in a number of rides and races and "scorched" her way to the front of the pack, well ahead of her white sisters, it was noted.

Despite her performance at the meet, Kittie still faced rejection on a daily basis by the townspeople of Asbury Park, who would not serve her at restaurants or allow her a room at the meet hotel. She was forced to stay in a boardinghouse at a distance from the other competitors.

When Kittie returned home to Boston, she was held up as a heroine in the cycling community. Her status was short-lived. Although she may have won the battle, she lost the war. In just a few years' time, even the local cycling clubs in and around Boston would disallow African Americans. By 1900, the cycling craze was fading. Unfortunately, Kittie may never have been aware of its demise; she died in 1900 at the age of only twenty-six years of kidney disease. Her grave was recently rededicated by her relatives in Mount Auburn Cemetery.

ANNIE "LONDONDERRY" KOPCHOVSKY

When Annie Kopchovsky heard about a wager between two Boston businessmen, she probably thought twice about it. And then some. She'd never been on a bike, let alone taken a trip of the size and scope these two were talking about: a woman bicycling around the world. Could she even leave her family for the months such an endeavor would take? The rules were daunting; she'd have to start with absolutely no money and accept no handouts. She'd have to earn $5,000 along the way and gain permission to visit over a dozen foreign countries. The two "clubmen" were clearly setting up a woman for failure, but the allure of $10,000 in prize money was just too great to not at least consider. Could she be the woman to best Thomas Stevens, a man who rode his bicycle around the world? In June 1894, she decided to find out.

Born in Latvia, she came to the United States with her family in 1875 at the age of four or five. The family settled in the West End, Boston's Jewish enclave. She married and stayed in the neighborhood, raising three children with her husband. There was nothing about her life or upbringing that would indicate, or even hint, that she would set out for a whirlwind tour of the world on a bicycle. Beyond the substantial prize winnings, her motivation is unknown. Despite being a novice at cycling, she was prepared to be entrepreneurial. A condition of the bet was that she earn her own keep throughout the journey and accept no handouts. Before she even set off on her trip, she was armed with photograph cards to autograph and sell along the way, as well as promises to lecture to the crowds of people she was assured would turn out to see her.

She was set to start her journey from the Massachusetts State House in Boston. More than five hundred supporters and well-wishers came to see her off. One key attendee was a representative from the Londonderry Lithia Spring Water Company, who gave her $100 to not only post an advertising placard for the product on her bicycle but also use the name "Annie Londonderry" throughout her trip. Cha-ching! Only $4,900 to go.

She took off from Boston and headed for New York City, by way of Providence. Her next steps were to cut across New York State through Rochester and Buffalo. She eventually arrived in Chicago, where she determined, for just a day, to quit. She'd spent four months getting only halfway across the United States and was facing wintertime and the Rockies. Something convinced her otherwise, though, and she started afresh, this time pedaling from Chicago back to New York and right on to a cruise liner headed for France. The challenge was on again.

From France, she traveled to Egypt. Then on through Jerusalem. Off to Yemen and then Sri Lanka. She banged through Singapore, Saigon and Hong Kong. She reported riding through Russia and then through Japan. She took a ship to San Francisco and made her way across the American Southwest to return to Chicago in the fifteen-month timeframe. Along the way, she claimed to have been attacked by highwaymen in Marseilles and held prisoner by the Japanese. It's not clear if some of her exploits were really true or embellished for her readers after the trip was over. Regardless of whatever tales she may have made taller, the inescapable truth is that her ride was extraordinary. Consider that she didn't switch to wearing the controversial bloomers until she set out from Chicago; she would have been in the long skirts and jackets thought to be appropriate for a woman. She wore those same long skirts day in and day out—wet in the rain, muddy and dirty the rest of the time. Even bloomers wouldn't have been that marked of an improvement, though they did help to ease her way and also garnered additional attention from a public held rapt by her adventures. She also came to appreciate indoor plumbing in ways few of us can imagine.

Her original bicycle was also much heavier than modern-day cycles. If she bogged down in muddy roads, she had to carry or push it, which must have been slow going indeed. In Chicago, she traded in her forty-two-pound Columbia bicycle for a Sterling cycle that was twenty pounds lighter.

She did manage to raise $5,000, mainly through selling her bike—and her person—as advertising space. Much like NASCAR drivers today, every inch of her clothing was covered in ads. The *Pittsburgh Chronicle-Telegraph* reported in 1895 that she was "dressed in a fancy costume with circulars and advertisements sewn all over her dress."

At the end of the day, she was wildly successful. She'd circumnavigated the globe (mostly) on a bike. After she returned to Boston from Chicago, she moved her family to New York City, where she became a writer. The *New York World* asked her to write a column called "The New Woman," the popular epithet for the new breed of outspoken women demanding the right to vote and heading the charge for prohibition. She wrote in her first article, "I am a journalist and 'a new woman,' if that term means that I believe I can do anything that any man can do." She had gone far in proving it.

MARY SARGENT HOPKINS

Mary Sargent Neal was born in Lynn, Massachusetts, in July 1847. As a young woman, she and her family moved to Nyack, New York, and it was there that she met and married her second husband, Charles Hopkins. They moved between Brooklyn and Boston until they finally settled in Boston in 1884. The pair became avid tricycling enthusiasts, taking tours with the Ladies' North Shore Tricycle Club all over Boston and up through the Cape Ann area. Mary started to write about the tours for a few bicycling journals, and a career was born. At first writing under the pseudonym of "Merrie Wheeler," she was a strong proponent of cycling for women, specifically as a way to enjoy exercise out of doors that could not only be healthy but also transformative for women. As Finison writes in his book *Boston's Cycling Craze, 1880–1900*, Mary found that she could effectively reach out to women by writing in women's journals, in addition to cycling magazines. In *Kitchen Magazine*, she wrote, "The wheel is today the greatest emancipator extant for women—women who are longing to be free from nervousness, sick-headache, and a train of other ills. Indeed, the bicycle for women deserves to

This poster from Columbia Bicycles from 1895 shows the correct upright posture for women to use while riding, if not impractical clothing. *Courtesy of the Trustees of the Boston Public Library.*

rank with the greatest inventions of the century." She didn't stop spreading the gospel of the cycle with writing; she spoke to women as a lecturer and presenter, and she socialized with the leading lights of the temperance and suffragist movements. However, this didn't necessarily mean that she was leading the charge for women's rights.

In 1895, she started her own journal called *The Wheelwoman*, publishing from an office on Tremont Street overlooking the Boston Common. She was the undisputed leader of women cyclists, and although she didn't necessarily discount equality for the sexes, her interest was much more founded on the basis of women's health and, ultimately, their beauty. Susan B. Anthony is famously quoted as saying, "Let me tell you what I think of bicycling. I think it has done more to emancipate women than anything else in the world. It gives women a feeling of freedom and self-reliance. I stand and rejoice every time I see a woman ride by on a wheel… the picture of free, untrammeled womanhood." Mary thought that health was more important than all other considerations in a woman's life, including education, and that bicycling was the best way to a healthy life. A healthy body by way of bicycling would "erase the tired looks in their eyes and the tense lines around their mouths."

Mary was fighting an uphill ride. Not everyone embraced bicycling for women. As sure as it was becoming a popular pastime in the middle and upper classes, it most surely had detractors. Publications lampooned women cyclists for being "Amazons"—in other words, unfeminine and unattractive. "Medical professionals" claimed that riding and such vigorous activity would ruin women's reproductive health—a claim that would not be put to rest until almost one hundred years later, when another wild woman ran the Boston Marathon. Furthermore, medical authorities believed that bicycling could lead women to experiment with unchaste behavior, partly due to the new fashion of going with dates on unchaperoned rides about town and partly in a more intimate manner due to straddling the bicycle seat. Talk about a hot-button issue!

But some things never change. Just as some of today's women feel conflicted about using the term "feminism" to describe their beliefs in equality for the sexes, Mary drew a line regarding how far she thought women should go. Bloomers or knickerbockers were far, far over the line for her. She told the *New York Times*, "If there is one thing I hate…it is a masculine woman. It has made my heart sore to see the women who have been putting on knickerbockers…and riding and scorching with the men. It has made wheeling just another way for a woman to make a fool of herself, bringing cycling into disrepute, and making herself the laughing stock of the people."

As bicycling grew ever more popular for women, so did the topic of what they should or could wear. Even Mary admitted that it was tough going to ride with the traditional long skirts and corsets of the day. She used her magazine to promote a new kind of adjustable skirt that could be made an appropriate length for daily wear and shortened for bike rides. Bloomers or knickerbockers were the answer for some. What could possibly be more threatening to society than pants on a woman? Women were pilloried in the press for wearing such "masculinizing" clothing. Men declared bloomers an abomination and vowed to not associate with women wearing them. Mary was firmly on their side.

So, despite being one of the most outspoken promoters of cycling for women, she never even mentioned Annie Kopchovsky's achievement of riding around the globe. Kittie Knox would get only dismissive remarks from Mary for what else but her "unseemly manner." Kittie Knox broke through the color line. Annie Kopchovsky took the ride of a lifetime. And Mary shook her head in disgust.

A black woman in a controversial costume daring to test the white establishment, a first-generation Jewish mother of three riding solo around the world and a strong-minded career woman—each of them was an outsider in her own ways. And each was a pioneer.

Chapter 11
NIGHTMARE NURSE
"Jolly" Jane Toppan

Amelia Phinney slipped in and out of consciousness. She'd just had a painful operation, and the world around her swam. Her breathing was shallow, and her eyes flickered open and shut as she tried to gain a grip on reality. As she lay in bed, she thought she felt a body being pressed against her. The warmth was at once comforting and disconcerting; she was being kissed over and over again. As she came to, she realized that this was not a dream—a woman was in her bed, pressing her face with kisses. She heard a door start to open, and the woman abruptly disentangled herself and left the room. Amelia breathed deeply with relief but soon fell asleep again, barely registering what had happened. When she awoke fully the next day, she wrote the experience off as a bad dream and forgot about it. Until twenty years later, when she read that nurse Jane Toppan had been arrested for the murder of at least thirty people under her care. She shuddered in terror as details of the murders emerged. And for good reason—as Jane's patient, she had been uncomfortably close to being one of her victims.

BEGINNINGS

Born in 1857, Honora Kelley and her sisters grew up under very rough conditions in Boston. Her mother died from tuberculosis when she was just a toddler, leaving the father to raise her and her sisters. Her father was a troubled man who was attached to the bottle and known around town as Kelley the Crack—as in crackpot. At one time, he worked as a tailor, and word on the street was that he once sewed his own eyelids shut. Honora and her older sister, Delia, likely suffered physical and mental abuse by their unstable father. He left them with the Boston Female Asylum on Washington Street in Boston's South End when Honora was six years old.

Honora was indentured as a servant by the Toppan family of Lowell at the age of seven. She lived with the family for many years, and although she was never formally adopted and certainly never accepted as an equal, she grew to love and feel close to the family to such an extent that she took their name and changed her name to Jane Toppan.

Jane's foster mother, Ann Toppan, who shared the widely held notion of the time that the Irish were below the bottom of the social ladder, never let Jane forget that she was of Irish heritage. Ann went so far as to tell friends of the family that Jane was an Italian immigrant whom the Toppan family had saved from the streets. So ashamed of her ethnic heritage, Jane herself looked down on and would make rude comments about people of Irish origin as she got older. Ann also reinforced Jane's insecurities regarding her origins and humiliated her at every opportunity. Jane responded by developing an outgoing and ingratiating personality. But even Jane's amazing capacity for spinning a tale was held up for critique by her foster mother, who claimed that Jane's "gift of gab" was a direct result of her Irishness. No matter what she did, Jane would always be inadequate in her foster mother's eyes.

Jane was raised with two other girls—Ann Toppan's daughters. Ann made no bones about calling out differences between them and Jane, making Jane miserable with envy. Seeing her foster sisters being treated with love and kindness while she was treated like a servant made her seethe. While her sisters were courted by eligible young men, Jane sat home, fantasizing about a romantic life but understanding that her chances of marriage were slim. Despite her intense jealousy, her sister Elizabeth treated her kindly, and the two got along well—for the time being.

At the age of eighteen, Jane was released from her indenture agreement and was paid the fifty dollars the family owed her. She decided to continue on with the family as a servant. Ann Toppan died shortly thereafter, leaving everything to her daughters—another slap in Jane's face. Just before Ann passed, Elizabeth married the Reverend Oramel Brigham, and she took over the house. Serving Elizabeth and her husband was too much for Jane to bear, so at the age of twenty-nine, it was time for Jane to set out on her own.

The Female Psychopath

A portrait of "Jolly" Jane Toppan at the time of her trial. *Courtesy of the Trustees of the Boston Public Library.*

At such a young age, it already seemed that things were falling in line for Jane to become a murderous psychopath: her traumatic childhood with familial mental illness, growing up neglected after coming from a broken home, the constant chorus of inadequacies sung out by her foster mother and the rejection of her ethnicity and family background by those who raised her, with virtually no nurturing figure in her young life. In order to escape harsh reality, Jane, like other psychopaths, developed a rich fantasy life.

Female serial killers typically kill in one of two ways—at home or at work. Often, they retain the traditional role of caretaker, which gives them the perfect opportunity to strike an unsuspecting victim. What these women have in common with their male counterparts is the need for control and power over their victim. All of these themes played out in the story of "Jolly Jane."

Sinister Seeds Are Sown

When Jane left to enter the workforce, she needed to choose a new profession. She trained to become a nurse, which was one of the few occupational opportunities afforded to her social class and gender. It was the perfect time and environment for her malevolent side to show itself.

She trained at the Cambridge Hospital in Boston, where she was beloved by the patients but not trusted by her coworkers. She seemed to have two personalities. With her patients, she was warm, effusive and caring, earning her the nickname "Jolly Jane." She used her gift of gab to her advantage, endearing her patients to her. On the other hand, she lied to her coworkers, started rumors and bad-mouthed others behind their backs, which did not exactly engender her colleagues' trust. They also suspected her of questionable ethics; she was thought to have been stealing, and she was suspected of altering some of her patients' medical charts. When she was confronted, she denied it all and appeared to be deeply offended at the suggestion.

It was at Cambridge Hospital that Jane started to experiment on patients with a mix of morphia and atropine, which would make patients violently ill and take them to the brink of death. Their symptoms would confuse doctors as to the underlying cause, and without exception, they misdiagnosed the patients, which enabled Jane to continue her experiments and, eventually, to kill patients. The symptoms themselves were horrible: spasms, uncontrollable picking at their skin and maniacal laughter. The way Jane administered the drugs was equally as horrifying. Most times she'd spike her victim's glass of mineral water, but often she'd use injections or even enemas. She enjoyed controlling her patients' reactions, but it went deeper than that—she controlled how long a patient might be in distress before she pulled them back to consciousness, and she controlled the usually all-powerful doctors, who had no idea what was afflicting these poor people. She was the smartest person in the room, pulling the strings of multiple puppets.

She often took her depravity to another level. When she was alone with the patients she was poisoning, she would get into bed with them so that she could feel them take their last breaths. Cleaving tightly to them as their breath became shallow and their bodies shuddered with pain, Jane felt a release of sexual energy. Jane was aroused by the pain she caused, the control she had over her patients. Unfortunately, there'd never be a second date.

Despite all this, Jane's supervisors at both the Cambridge Hospital and, later, Massachusetts General Hospital loved her. When she decided to go out on her own to work in private care, making a much bigger paycheck, they lined up to give her excellent recommendations. Now, she'd be under no one's watchful eyes, and she could kill at will. And she did.

IT'S PERSONAL

From 1892 to 1900, Jane was reputedly the most successful private nurse in Cambridge, working all over the Boston area. In private practice, she developed a penchant for disposing of not just her patients but also people like her landlords, Israel and Lovey Dunham, who began to grate on her over time. She did away with poor Israel because he was getting "fussy" but then continued to live in the Dunham home—until two years later, when she dispatched Lovey for the same reason. Then Jane moved on, with no remorse. For Jane, killing was personal, as Jane's foster sister Elizabeth would learn all too soon.

Jane and Elizabeth were never close, but Elizabeth treated Jane with respect and an open heart. Jane would take summer trips to Cape Cod, and in August 1899, she invited Elizabeth to come along. Just like two sisters, they picnicked by the ocean, catching up with each other. No one understood why Elizabeth fell into a coma after her day at the beach—and how she could possibly die a day later.

It was again on Cape Cod, in the town of Cataumet, that Jane finally went too far.

Jane rented a small cottage from the Davis family every year. She had a great relationship with them, but she'd occasionally run a little low on making a full payment. Over time, the debt accumulated, and Mattie Davis decided to make a collection call to Jane's home. As it happened, Mattie's daughter, Minnie, would be making the trip back home to Boston from Chicago, and Mattie could meet her train. Mattie's trip started inauspiciously, as she suffered a nasty fall on her way to the train. Fortunately for her, other than being terribly shaken and nursing a bruised ego, she was fine.

However, when Jane and Mattie met, Jane seized upon the news of Mattie's terrible tumble and immediately offered her a glass of cool mineral water. Unfortunately for Mattie, it was loaded with morphia. When the two made their way to the bank to collect the back rent, Mattie collapsed, and Jane's reign of terror began. Jane kept Mattie slipping into and out of consciousness—first giving her family hope of survival and then driving them to the depths of despair. Mattie finally lapsed into a coma and died, but not without Jane slipping into bed with her, holding Mattie close as she took her last breath.

Always so loving and considerate, Jane accompanied the family back to Cataumet for the funeral. The two remaining Davis daughters, Genvieve and Minnie, asked her to stay as their guest out of appreciation for all that Jane had done for their mother in her dying days. Little did they know that they'd be next.

By now, Jane had truly gone off the proverbial deep end. Before trying her usual methods to kill the Davis family, she tried to incinerate them. She made no fewer than three attempts to burn down their house with the family still inside. When that failed, she turned her attention to Genvieve. She took Minnie aside and spun a tale about her suspicion that Genvieve might try to commit suicide, since, by Jane's account, she had witnessed Genvieve fingering a box of poison. The two kept watch. Indeed, Genvieve was depressed, but suicide was something too rash to consider—or was it? Certainly, Jane wasn't surprised when Genvieve got sick after dinner—or when she never recovered. Jane's aim then focused on Alden Davis, husband of Mattie and patriarch of the Davis family.

Alden was also obviously wasted by the recent loss of his wife and young daughter in the span of just a few weeks, but life went on. After he returned to Cape Cod from a trip to Boston, he was feeling tired. Jane greeted him with her usual cocktail, a nice cool glass of mineral water, and the next morning, Alden was dead. Four days later, Minnie joined her family in their seaside grave.

While many thought it was certainly plausible that the family had a run of terrible, tragic luck, four deaths in the span of two months finally led at least two people to be suspicious: Captain Paul Gibbs, the local police authority (and the late Minnie's father-in-law), and a Boston doctor, Ira Cushing, who'd not only read about the tragedy in the newspaper but also observed Alden on his recent train ride. Dr. Cushing had been struck by how healthy Alden seemed. Although both Gibbs and Cushing wrote off their hunches, a mutual friend of the two made it clear that they might be on to something. They decided to involve the authorities.

THE END

A Harvard toxicologist, Dr. Edward S. Wood, was asked to undertake an investigation, ordering the exhumation of Genvieve and Minnie. At that time, Jane was back in Boston, about to try to pull off her next, even more twisted plan. She was determined to capture the heart of Oramel Brigham, her dead foster sister's husband. Unfortunately, and very inconveniently, Oramel's seventy-seven-year-old sister, Edna, was in town when Jane arrived to make her play. Fortunately, Edna was easily dispatched with barely a second thought.

Oramel wisely rejected Jane's advances, and in a pathetic attempt at revenge, she attempted to commit suicide by poisoning herself with morphia. Proving less successful with suicide than homicide, she was recovering at a friend's home in New Hampshire when she was finally arrested in October 1901 for the poisoning deaths of the Davis family.

Over the course of the next months, Jane's deeds were made public and played out across international newspapers. Jane would eventually be declared criminally insane and sentenced to life in prison. When asked about her crimes, she exhibited no remorse at all and recounted them in clinical detail. "Her motive?" asked the authorities. Her answer rocked the questioners—purely for sexual satisfaction.

She lived out the remainder of her eighty-one years in the Taunton (Massachusetts) Insane Asylum, where she lived in fear of being poisoned to death.

Chapter 12
THE BELLE EPOQUE

Isabella Stewart Gardner

*T*he Gardners walked into the artist's London studio, pleased to meet the new young talent. This was especially true for the missus, since she had taken an interest in collecting art and made it her business to know of all the most promising up-and-comers. She especially liked it if the art and the artist had the whiff of controversy around them. And this one fit the bill. Big time. The painting she and her husband had come to the studio to see had just caused a furor in Paris—a furor so big that the artist had abandoned his Paris studio, taking the painting with him, in shame and indignation. It was one of his best works, now considered a masterpiece. But at the time, the portrait of Madame Gautreau was scandalous, as much for her self-assured gaze as her bare shoulder and décolletage. He called it *Madame X*.

There's no such thing as bad press, which Mrs. Gardner knew well, and in London, John Singer Sargent had reestablished a successful studio painting portraits of high society's women after a cooling-off period. It was no surprise, then, when Mrs. Gardner quickly established a friendship with him. She'd mentored many young artists and was building a world-class art collection. She knew talent when she saw it. A year later, Sargent came to Boston to paint her portrait. Given Isabella's penchant for upsetting the apple cart, was there ever any doubt that Mr. Gardner, after the initial public viewing, would ask that his wife's portrait never again see the light of day? Would she have had it any other way?

BEGINNINGS

Isabella Stewart was born on April 14, 1840, and was raised in New York City. She married John "Jack" Gardner of Boston, a wealthy and well-connected businessman, on April 10, 1860. She moved to Boston and settled, first, at the Hotel Boylston after living with her in-laws. Located at the corner of Boylston and Tremont Streets, it wasn't a hotel as we conceive it today but a French flat, a cutting-edge living experiment for the rich that usually housed one family per floor, with the servants toward the back of the property and kitchen in the basement. In 1866, the couple moved into a five-story brownstone in the newly developed Back Bay at 152 Beacon Street. (The building was demolished in 1902.)

When Isabella first arrived in Boston, she was snubbed by the other society women. Despite being from the bigger and more fashionable city of New York, she wasn't from an established family with a long list of ancestors who bounded off the *Mayflower* and never left. Boston Brahmins were known for being reserved in manner and dress, and Isabella just didn't fit in. She wasn't really interested in fitting in. Reflecting on that later, she said she didn't mind; she liked men better anyway. Men returned the favor, which was, perhaps, part of the problem. When she was shunned by her female peers, it worked to her advantage because young men took pity on her, asking her to dance. It wasn't pity for long, though, as she charmed them and wowed them with her fancy footwork. It all worked in her favor and created an air of rumors around her about the men in her life. People liked to talk, and Isabella let them.

She seemed to magnetically draw scandal, and rather than change her ways to bow to society, she owned it. In fact, she cultivated it. She was always her own person; she owned her storyline. And there were stories. The press loved to write about her. People loved to read about her. Brahmins were shocked, and she just laughed.

She counted among her closest friends the leading lights of the Boston intelligentsia, the movers and shakers. And although she could hold her own with close friend and suffragette Julia Ward Howe and novelist and poet Sarah Orne Jewett, as well as well-known males like the author Henry James and master artists John Singer Sargent and James MacNeill Whistler, she knew how to mix it up, too.

Expect the Unexpected

As recounted in the biography *Mrs. Jack* by Louise Hall Tharp, Isabella organized a prizefight for "an exclusive audience of Boston society women." The boxing match was held in a studio on Tremont Street filled with statuary and furniture that all needed to be cleared out to make space for the boxing ring. Referee Jack Sheean was shocked when the audience of proper female Bostonians started to cheer, and he was perhaps more surprised when no one fainted or left the room during the seventeen-round fight.

Her society peers, after rejecting Isabella in those early days, learned to appreciate her wild side and looked to her to organize such mischief. She apparently invited another prizefighter to pose shirtless behind a screen in her home to greet women as they entered. At some point, all agreed that the screen was unnecessary

The imposing Isabella Stewart Gardner.
Courtesy of the Trustees of the Boston Public Library.

and took in the sight of the finely muscled fighter in all his glory. And we thought the "ladies who lunch" only got together to have tea and finger sandwiches! Who knew that the Chippendales they spoke of were in addition to their furniture!

Isabella was so well known among prizefighters that, according to legend, as she was making her way back to the Back Bay from a dinner in South Boston in a hired carriage, she was caught up in a crowd of angry streetcar workers. The crowd seized on her elegant coach and most likely would not have missed seeing the opulent jewelry she was wearing. She was, after all, known for mounting two giant diamonds on springs and wearing them in her hair. As the crowd grew nearer and more dangerous, a man emerged from the mob and approached the cab. It was none other than the Boston Strong Boy, first heavyweight champion and bare-knuckle boxer, John L. Sullivan, who had come to her rescue. True or not, it makes for good telling.

ARTFUL DODGER

Isabella is known today mainly for her incredible art collection and unparalleled art museum on Boston's Fenway. So it would make sense that stories would arise that even her collection, esteemed as it was, grew by trickery and mischief, but maybe they are just that—only stories. It could be that some of the masterpieces she acquired were bought not just by her checkbook and good eye but by use of a little cleverness, maybe a bit of guile and a fast get-away carriage.

Isabella was friendly with many artists, and James MacNeill Whistler was but one of many. Visiting his studio in Paris, she spotted a painting that she wanted badly, but he refused to sell it. The painting was called *Harmony in Blue and Silver*. She didn't let Whistler's refusal to sell get in her way. The story goes that she hoodwinked her cousin, Thomas Jefferson Coolidge, into coming along with her to Whistler's studio one afternoon. She asked him to "take a certain picture down to the carriage without a fuss." Sounded simple enough. While Isabella created a distraction, Coolidge grabbed and ran. One version of the story has Whistler chasing the two out of the studio, only to sign the painting in resignation before she took off with it. Yet another version keeps the chase scene but ends with Isabella refusing Whistler the opportunity to add his signature, requiring him to lunch with her at her hotel, where, with the painting firmly in her possession, he was free to sign it away. Yet another, much more boring, version exists, but it's quite possibly the true version, and that is that her husband simply bought it. But as she is quoted as saying, "Don't spoil a good story by telling the truth." Regardless of how she obtained it, the painting can be viewed in the building she designed as her home and museum, Fenway Court.

She was equally desperate to acquire a painting called *El Jaleo*. A dramatic painting by John Singer Sargent, it shows a Spanish gypsy dancer in front of a group of musicians; you can practically hear the dancer's shoes rapping the floorboards when you first see it, largely because of the way Isabella staged the painting. It's almost twelve feet wide and is displayed in a room especially designed for it. How did it get there? Thomas Jefferson Coolidge, her cousin and alleged accomplice in the Whistler caper, had owned *El Jaleo* since it was painted in 1882 and promised it to Isabella in his will. But judging by the alleged events with the Whistler painting, when it came to denying Isabella's wishes, Coolidge never had a chance. So why should she hedge her bets when she had just the place for this painting? She went ahead and designed a room in Fenway Court called the Spanish Cloister especially for the masterwork. The lighting was tended to; other objects that would complement the painting were placed in the room. It was perfect. She took the painting "on loan," and once Coolidge saw it in this special setting, there was no question that the painting belonged there. It has been there ever since.

Portrait of a Lady

And what of that never-to-be-viewed-by-the-public portrait of Isabella painted by John Singer Sargent? Isabella sat for Sargent in January 1888. It was one of his more difficult commissions; Isabella would not sit still. He threatened to give up, but she insisted that he continue to try. They were both glad that he did. The result was what Isabella thought was one of Sargent's best portraits—of anyone, ever.

It is a full-length view, capturing Isabella standing quietly in a simple black dress with a rope of pearls around her waist. She greets the viewer directly but demurely. The background is rich and, some say, recalls circular halos surrounding Isabella's head. She holds her hands down in front of her. There is a sense of calm. Despite Isabella's playful personality, the painting is not at all dramatic. So what of the controversy? The neckline was low. Not outrageously low, but then again, that might depend on who you asked. When the painting was shown at the fashionably elegant St. Botolph Club on Newbury Street, which was composed of gentlemen interested in the arts, Mr. Gardner overheard some members taking a gander at his wife's portrait and declaring that they could "see all the way down to Crawford's Notch!" That was enough for Jack. He knew they weren't talking about the White Mountains of New Hampshire! The painting was never shown publicly again until after her death, which was well after Jack's.

It is also said that when Mr. Gardner saw the painting, he said to Isabella, "It looks like hell, but it looks like you." So Jack knew how to play, too.

Patronizing

Despite all the fun and games, Isabella's legacy looms large over the Boston landscape—both physically and culturally. She was one of the first to build in the newly reclaimed marshland area the Fens. Designed by Frederick Law Olmsted as a park that would look like a "wild" seaside meadow, the Fenway is now home to multiple cultural institutions. The Boston Museum of Fine Arts (MFA) went out on a limb and laid its claim to the neighborhood in 1895, buying a large tract of land. But when push came to shove, Isabella still beat it to the punch by six years. Ever ahead of the times, she opened Fenway Court in January 1903, while the MFA did not open until 1909.

Over years of trips to Europe and Asia, Isabella and her husband collected art. They filled their home in the Back Bay, even after they had doubled its size by buying and then expanding into the neighboring building. They considered building a new home, but plans were abruptly halted when Mr. Gardner died unexpectedly of a stroke in 1896. Isabella, as so often was the case, decided on a wholly new direction—to build in the Fenway. She also

A view of Fenway Court from the as-yet-undeveloped Fenway neighborhood of Boston. The setting heightens the effect of the building being a Venetian palace. *Courtesy of the Trustees of the Boston Public Library.*

An interior view of Fenway Court just after it opened. *Courtesy of the Trustees of the Boston Public Library.*

determined to not build just any typical town house but something she'd dreamed of ever since she visited Venice, Italy, for the first time as a girl. She built a Venetian palace that is, to this day, unlike any building in the Boston area. She hired noted architects Cummings and Sears but was intimately involved in the design and construction of the building, making regular visits to the construction site.

Called Fenway Court, the building features a garden-filled central courtyard surrounded on all four sides by galleries opening up to rooms. The villa was opened to the public as a museum almost immediately. She kept private rooms on the fourth floor. Today, the museum is a showcase of over 2,500 paintings, sculptures, tapestries, furniture, rare manuscripts and books and includes works by the aforementioned John Singer Sargent and James MacNeill Whistler, as well as Botticelli, Titian and Rembrandt.

The interior of the main museum remains unchanged, according to her wishes. (A new wing was opened in 2012 to provide additional program and gallery space.) No paintings are ever loaned to other museums, nor are any shown here that were not on display during Isabella's lifetime. Holding to tradition, the museum staff also places a vase of violets below one of her favorite paintings, *Christ Carrying the Cross* by Giovanni Bellini, as she often did. Also left unchanged are a few reminders of her fun and quirky personality; for instance, as an ardent Red Sox fan, she's guaranteed that those coming to the museum in Red Sox gear receive discounted tickets. And always one to take care of her own, anyone named Isabella is celebrated with free lifetime admission.

END TO THE BEAUTIFUL ERA

Isabella was eighty-four years old when she died after a series of strokes in 1924. But she ensured that her love of art, beauty and appreciation of tradition would carry on even after her death by endowing her museum with $1 million and making large gifts to several local charities in her will. Beyond the expected allocations, there is an unexpected request. All of Isabella's supposed transgressions and head-turning lifestyle notwithstanding, every year on her birthday, a Requiem Mass is held in her honor at Fenway Court. It is a small and private ceremony held in the chapel on the property. She is buried in Mount Auburn Cemetery.

Chapter 13
FOR THE BIRDS

Harriet Hemenway and Minna Hall

On a chilly January day in 1896, a woman sat in her well-appointed town house on Clarendon Street in the heart of Boston's fashionable Back Bay neighborhood, held rapt by what she was reading. What she learned sickened her. Then it made her angry. Collecting her thoughts and the article, she hurried across the street to share it with her friend. Together, they absorbed the enormity of the task they were about to take on and sat down to plot a plan of action. In the end, they would take down a multimillion-dollar industry, create one of our country's most enduring institutions and kick off the environmental conservation movement in the United States. When Harriet Hemenway and Minna Hall set their minds to do something, nothing—and no one—stood in their way. Their wings were made to fly.

HATS OFF!

In 1896, hats had been fashionable for both men and women for years. The then-popular practice of decorating them with feathers, which dates back to antiquity, reached its zenith in the late 1800s, when ladies' hats became incredibly elaborate and sumptuous. They reflected a trend in the culture toward all things natural and featured not only feathers but also flowers, butterflies, nests, leaves, grass and even whole taxidermied birds. Frank Chapman, an ornithologist from the American Museum of Natural History,

This trade card shows a hat with entire taxidermied birds along the top. The hat is called "The Myra." The card was produced by the Hills Brothers of New York City, circa 1870–1900. *Courtesy of the Trustees of the Boston Public Library.*

counted forty different species of birds on women's hats in the span of just two afternoon walks in New York City.

The popularity of these hats fueled an entire industry—not just of hat making but also the cruel work of harvesting the plumage of a wide variety of birds. A good deal of money was made. In the early 1900s, the plumes of herons and egrets were worth $32 an ounce. Adjusting for inflation, an ounce of feathers would be worth $770 today! The harvesting was devastating to bird life across the United States. In 1886, the American Ornithologists' Union, an early precursor to the Audubon Society, estimated that five million birds a year were killed just for decorating hats—an unsustainable number by any measure and one that makes one wonder how more species didn't become extinct.

Still, with such big stakes in the millinery business at the time, the owners of those businesses circled the wagons to protect themselves. They claimed that their feathers were not taken from birds they killed but that the feathers had naturally molted—left on the ground for the milliners to pick up and use. A more disingenuous statement could not be made; this simply was not the case. Molting alone could never have produced the tremendous number of feathers needed to fuel the industry. Birds were brutally killed in vast numbers, and their young were left to die starving beside them.

This was what Harriet Hemenway had been reading about on that January day—an account of an entire rookery in Florida being decimated—and she felt called to do something about it. She and her friend and cousin Minna Hall hatched a plan and set immediately to work.

RUFFLING FEATHERS

Harriet Lawrence Hemenway was born into one of Boston's most elite families, and when she married Augustus Hemenway Jr., she secured her station. Augustus Jr. came from a long line of well-heeled men and spent much of his life in philanthropy, never having to work. Harriet's father was himself a firebrand who put his money where his mouth was. A.A. Lawrence's fortune was made in the textile mill trade. The former mill town of Lawrence, Massachusetts, is named after him, as is Lawrence, Kansas, which was founded as a free-soil (antislave) town. Lawrence was on the leading edge of the abolition movement and supported efforts to keep slavery out of Kansas. Both families were not just reform-minded but also

The home of Harriet Hemenway on Clarendon Street in Boston's Back Bay. *Photo by Dina Vargo.*

deeply engaged in a number of important movements and gave liberally to cultural institutions like museums, libraries and symphonies in Boston.

Supporting a cause came naturally to Harriet, who was rather outspoken and unafraid to take on convention. For example, in her portrait painted by the noted society artist John Singer Sargent, she's holding a water lily. While we make nothing of that today, at the time it was scandalous; the water lily symbolized pregnancy, and this was her way of making a private announcement very public.

Never one to back off a controversy, she once ruffled feathers by opening her home to an African American man when no others in Boston would offer him a place to stay. The man was Booker T. Washington, who was to become a nationally known educator and civil rights leader.

Harriet and Minna had enjoyed wearing feathered hats, fashionable ladies that they were, but once a bell is rung, it can't be undone. The graphic article that they read detailing the slaughter of birds in Florida was all the convincing that either one of them needed to take action.

Harriet and Minna were not the only monied and well-intentioned women in Boston. They had friends and they had connections. They decided to use them and, combined with the structure of society, create an organization to fight the hunters supplying the millinery factories with the feathers of slaughtered birds.

The plan consisted of various marketing and public relations strategies. First, they consulted the *Boston Blue Book*, a listing of all of Boston's blue-blooded Brahmins, and invited the women for tea and discussion at Harriet's Back Bay home. This started a series of tea meetings held all over Greater Boston, and the meetings resulted in more than nine hundred women signing on to protect helpless birds from being turned into the latest look.

Despite all their energy, money and commitment, the ladies knew that the only way for their movement to gain any traction was to attain the buy-in of men. The only way to do that was to hand over the leadership of their movement—if in name only. They turned to the American Ornithologists' Union (AOU), which had the same goal as Harriet's informal group but took a more scientific tack. So while the AOU had scientific credentials on its side, it, unlike the ladies, had no grassroots support. Harriet proposed something of a merger and formed a new organization called the Massachusetts Audubon Society, after the famous painter John Audubon. She chose William Brewster, a noted Harvard ornithologist and co-founder of the AOU, to be the group's leader. The new organization immediately found its voice and became a major player nationally. Very early in its creation, it was determined to set up similar organizations in other states, like Pennsylvania, Connecticut and New York, to expand its network, share its vision and strengthen its strategy.

In short order, they were able to win passage of legislation in Massachusetts to outlaw the trade of feathers. Later, the bill would be used as a model for national legislation called the Lacey Act, which was passed in 1900. In 1913 and 1916, two more acts of legislation were passed nationally to protect migratory birds, and an agreement with Great Britain was struck to do the same.

Bring On the Girls

Another winning strategy Harriet and the society employed was to make this battle for and about women. Just as the women sought out male scientists to legitimize their work, the men had to admit that the only way to really stop the feather trade was to appeal to women—they, after all, bought and wore the feathered hats. Because birds of a feather flock together, one of the strongest parts of their strategy was to recruit fashionable women who publicly rejected such hats. Predictably, the middle and working classes quickly followed along.

Harriet and Minna were also not afraid to take on some very important people. Minna was tasked by Harriet to write a letter to First Lady Helen Taft, admonishing her for wearing feathers at her husband's inauguration in 1909. These ladies weren't just classy, they were brassy.

They also saw to it that women played a role in the organization's leadership. Eighteen of the forty officers of the Massachusetts Audubon Society were women. Included were Julia J. Irvine, the president of Wellesley College, and Elizabeth Cary Agassiz, the president of Radcliffe College, both exclusively women's colleges.

Women had yet another role—as members of local chapters. Another part of Harriet's and Minna's brilliant strategy for growing support for their cause was giving people, especially women and children, a way to get involved. By 1897, there were 111 local chapters in Massachusetts, and 105 of those were led by women. Because many of these women were teachers, they enlisted the help and attention of schoolchildren who would themselves become involved in the future, sustaining the organization for years to come.

Still, the millinery trade made up a significant part of the economy, employing one in every one thousand Americans. In response to the society boycott of feathered hats, the millinery business claimed that these laws would damage the United States economy, which would prove to be like Chicken Little exclaiming that the sky was falling. Some legislators believed the threats, and some even believed that birds were put on this earth to adorn the hats of lovely ladies. Ultimately, these views were on the wrong side of history. By the 1920s, the feather trade was dead.

Taking Flight

Harriet and Minna stayed involved in the Audubon Society for the rest of their lives, as did many of the social elites they recruited at the organization's inception. When they were well into their eighties and celebrating the fiftieth anniversary of the Massachusetts Audubon Society, Minna said that Harriet "doesn't know when to stop," and indeed, Harriet kept taking on causes in a variety of ways. During World War I, she operated a canning kitchen in the rear of her home and sold the proceeds to benefit veterans. She backed the cause of working women by teaching classes at the Women's Education and Industrial Union, an organization founded in Boston in the late nineteenth century for the advancement of women and children.

Neither did either woman ever grow tired of exploring the outdoors, often with their children and grandchildren in tow. Minna spent time walking around Hall's Pond off Beacon Street in Brookline, a piece of land her family previously owned that, coincidentally, became the first conservation land bought by the Town of Brookline in 1975. Harriet, always the iconoclast, often made tracks in a pair of less-than-fashionable white sneakers she later grew famous for wearing.

Minna died in 1951 at the age of 92, and Harriet stuck around until the ripe old age of 102 in 1960.

Chapter 14
THE BLONDE WITCH OF BEACON HILL

Mina "Margery" Crandon

*B*eacon Hill was (and still is) filled with Boston's most proper and monied citizens, called Brahmins by Oliver Wendell Holmes to indicate their higher social status. It was also home to one woman who may have been less traditionally accomplished than her neighbors but celebrated nonetheless. She was quite possibly the world's best-known medium, believed to contact the dead with the help of her deceased brother, Walter, as her spirit guide.

On a summer day in 1924, she and her husband were anxiously awaiting a not-altogether-desired guest at their home at 10 Lime Street. The two looked at each other with nervous excitement; they knew their claims would be put to the test. There was no doubt in Dr. Le Roy Crandon's mind that his wife, Mina, or, as the press called her, "Margery," would succeed in proving to the world that her gifts were real. His faith in his wife knew no bounds—which was appropriate, considering that her gift involved reaching beyond the boundaries of the known world and into the spiritual world.

Articles had been written about her paranormal powers, and the two had accepted a challenge made by *Scientific American* magazine to prove to the world that Mina was no ten-cent sideshow attraction. Other observers disagreed, however, and it was time to put Mina's gifts to the test.

The two startled when the bell rang, and their servant announced that their guest had arrived: "Sir. Madam. Harry Houdini is here."

EARTHBOUND BEGINNINGS

Mina Crandon was born in Ontario, Canada, where her parents managed a farm. She moved to Boston as a young woman to play in local bands and orchestras. She eventually became a secretary at the Union Congregational Church and met her first husband, Earl Rand, a grocer. They married in 1910 and had a son together. She met Dr. Crandon, a surgeon fifteen years her senior, at a hospital in Dorchester, Massachusetts; they later reconnected during World War I, when she served as a volunteer ambulance driver and he acted as the head of surgical staff at the New England Naval Hospital. A few months later, in 1918, Mina filed for divorce and quickly married Dr. Crandon, becoming his third wife.

Dr. Crandon, a haughty, snobbish Boston Brahmin, was also deeply interested in the occult. At the time, this was not extraordinary. Immediately after World War I, there was a resurgence in a movement called Spiritualism, whose adherents believed in the afterlife and put great stock in the ability to connect to spirits for guidance. The movement started in 1848 when two sisters in upstate New York began rapping out—handclapping in code—messages from the dead. The Fox sisters became a sensation, and the Spiritualist religion grew up around their ability to communicate with unseen spirits, rapping out answers to questions in a simplistic "clap one for yes, two for no" style. In time, more mediums would emerge with various ways of communicating with spirits; some were gifted, and others were pure hucksters, as séances both private and public became all the rage. Some mediums, most of whom were women, demanded excessively high fees for their appearances, and the trade-off was more and more scrutiny. Some mediums were found to be outrageous frauds. People became more wary and demanded hard proof of their claims, especially if they were paying top dollar. Mina Crandon discovered her gifts at just this time.

Dr. Crandon's interest in the occult led him to read a book on the topic, and he was particularly taken with the tale of a table that floated on air, seemingly directed by spirits. In 1923, he decided to try to replicate the paranormal happening at his own home, constructing a table to the specifications listed in the book, and he asked some friends to attend the séance. To everyone's amazement, the table took flight! Who among them had the gift to channel spirits to move the table? After some experimentation, it was found to be none other than Mina. A career was born.

MEDIUM WELL

Mina was an especially gifted medium. Anything that Dr. Crandon read about, Mina could later reproduce. Objects seemingly floated through darkened rooms. A pigeon appeared out of nowhere. Lights flashed. Despite Mina filling her mouth with water, her voice still rang out. She became a sensation in Beacon Hill, hosting séances on the fourth floor of 10 Lime Street night after night. Dr. Crandon thought it was important for Mina to have a spirit guide as a grounding influence and suggested that she should be hypnotized to make contact with a helpful ancestor. During the trance, a man's voice came forth, using rather salty language. It was Mina's brother, Walter Stinson, manifesting himself to help Mina on her journey between worlds.

Before long, Mina became an international celebrity, and the press dubbed her "Margery" to help protect her identity. Her husband was so convinced of her talents that he took her abroad, where they met Sir Arthur Conan Doyle, well known as the creator of the detective Sherlock Holmes. Doyle was also regarded as an expert in the psychic and paranormal, and he became a huge fan and supporter, singing Mina's praises among the intelligentsia.

Around the same time, *Scientific American* magazine was involved in trying to determine the legitimacy of psychic claims. In 1922, it offered a prize of $2,500 to the first person who could "produce a visible psychic manifestation of other character…to the full satisfaction of these judges." A commission of judges was appointed to investigate all claims for the prize and included Sir Arthur Conan Doyle; William McDougall, a Harvard professor; Walter Franklin Prince, a psychic researcher; Dr. Daniel Frost Comstock, an MIT physicist and engineer; Hereward Carrington, an amateur magician and manager of a well-known Italian medium, Eusapia Palladino; and Harry Houdini, magician, escape artist and debunker of mediums.

Mina was a frontrunner to win the prize after an initial meeting with most of the commission, although some were as taken with her looks as with her talents. Mina was a modern beauty—blonde, bobbed hair and blue eyes. She was a charmer. Malcolm Bird, the secretary for the committee and staffer on the *Scientific American*, was entirely caught up in the magic of Mina. Committee members even stayed at the Crandons' home, giving a sense of impropriety to the proceedings.

One person was not buying the claims of Mina's fans, and he found the committee's behavior less than impartial. That was Harry Houdini, who was mysteriously left out of the committee's initial discoveries. It didn't take a psychic to discover why.

GHOSTBUSTER

Harry Houdini, as the son of a rabbi, was inclined toward spiritual thinking and in his youth explored the paranormal. He believed, or wanted to believe, in the power that mediums had but was frankly disappointed most times and

Houdini's life's work was exposing fraudulent mediums like Margery Crandon, as this poster made around 1909 shows. *Library of Congress Prints and Photographs Division Online Catalogue.*

could easily figure out their tricks. Early in Houdini's career, he and his wife acted as mediums while he was establishing himself as a magician, but they stopped after he realized how unethical it was to take advantage of the audience's emotional vulnerability. It was one thing to use sleight of hand to break out of handcuffs but another entirely to trick an innocent person into believing something as emotionally potent as receipt of messages from a dead loved one. So although he stopped, he continued to search for a truly gifted medium—especially after his mother died. He very much wanted to contact her.

Houdini and Arthur Conan Doyle were friends united in their quest to learn more about the spiritual world. Doyle was perhaps too gullible; Houdini tried to convince him that he himself had no special talents, that everything he did was a trick. But to Doyle, ignorance was bliss. It was more meaningful to him to keep his faith in the paranormal. Doyle arranged for Houdini to have a private session with a clairvoyant Doyle felt was the real deal, but time and again, the medium failed to deliver any reliable information from Houdini's mother. While Doyle was impressed by the woman's act, Houdini became more and more quiet. He didn't want to upset his friend, but he knew the medium was a fraud. Later, guided by his conscience, he told Doyle that he no longer put stock in these psychics, and the two had a huge falling out, from which they'd never recover.

With an idea of what to look for, Houdini started to expose fraudulent mediums as part of his life's work. He was especially galled that Mina might bilk the magazine of $2,500, being nothing but a trickster, and he felt protective of the vulnerable public whom many mediums were cheating. He was now entirely focused on taking Mina, and others like her, down.

Houdini sat with Mina for the first time on July 23, 1924, and ascertained a sense of what tricks were up her sleeve to produce her effects. She was able to ring a bell, send a megaphone flying across the room and project the voice of Walter. On their second meeting, Houdini came prepared, with what was known as the "Margery Box" to prove her a fake.

THE MARGERY BOX

The Margery Box was prepared and built by Houdini to entrap Mina, both literally and figuratively. It was a full-sized box that would allow her to sit, but with only her head and hands able to move and be seen. Houdini knew that Mina was achieving her metaphysical results by basic sleight of hand, with the aid of her husband as accomplice and the cover of darkness. If she couldn't move her feet, she couldn't ring the bell on the floor. If she couldn't move her arms, she wouldn't be able to place the megaphone on her head. If she couldn't move her head, she wouldn't be able to put her head underneath the table to send it flying. Despite all of Houdini's elaborate precautions, Mina still found a way to cheat.

An extendable carpenter's ruler was found inside the Margery Box later, and Mina, by maneuvering that ruler with her hand that should have been held tight by her husband, was still able to ring the bell located on the floor between Houdini's feet. When the ruler was found, Mina claimed that it had been planted there. At that point, Houdini proclaimed the whole proceeding an outrage.

Walter, Mina's brother who allegedly was protecting her from the other side, sang a little ditty about Mina's new nemesis:

> *Harry Houdini, he sure is a Sheeny*
> *A man with a crook in his shoe*
> *Says he, "As to Walter, I'll lead him to slaughter."*
> *"But," says Walter, "Perhaps I'll get you!"*

After more and more testing, in November 1924, the *Scientific American* committee ruled against Mina. Houdini called her an outright fraud, while the others were a bit more judicious in their words, saying that the testing lacked scientific controls or that, although she had exhibited some paranormal talent, it was not sufficient to win the prize. One member, the amateur magician Hereward Carrington, sat on the fence. Regardless of Mina's psychic gifts, Carrington may have had a few other reasons to stay on the good side of the Crandons—there was a rumor that he owed Dr. Crandon money, and he later claimed to have been having an affair with Mina at the time.

Houdini would spend the rest of his days showing the world the exact tactics Mina and others used to dupe people, even debunking her at a performance at Boston's Symphony Hall in January 1925. Mina continued on as usual, performing as a medium for years after. There was just too much public interest in the topic, and she had friends in high places; J. Malcolm Bird would go on to become the president of the American Society for Psychic Research and write a book called *"Margery" the Medium*.

Over the years, Mina's feats became more and more complex. She started to produce ectoplasm from her body, a gelatinous substance that was supposedly a spiritual residue. No one could quite uncover where it was coming from. Some astute observers thought that it looked remarkably like animal lung tissue, which her husband could easily spirit away from the hospital where he worked.

She eventually generated an ectoplasmic hand that would emerge from under her robe, under which she wore nothing but her birthday suit. The hand was motionless, cool and moist to the touch. Again, observers noted that it looked less like something spiritually produced than like something far more mundane: sculpted chicken livers. But these feats still stumped and amazed most of her audiences.

She finally overstepped the boundaries of credibility when she claimed to have been able to capture the fingerprint of her spirit guide and brother, Walter, in a piece of wax. Upon examination, however, it was found to be the fingerprint of her dentist—the man who gave her the wax and taught her how to make a fingerprint in it. It was not only disingenuous, it was lazy!

By now, people were catching on to Mina's tricks. When her husband died in 1939, she no longer had her greatest supporter or co-conspirator. Her career went into steep decline. She started to drink heavily, admitting that she carried a heavy weight of trying to give her audience more and more amazing experiences. She kept up for years, but it would never be enough.

Finally, the drinking and stress caught up to her. On November 1, 1941, Mina Crandon passed into the beyond. No one has heard a word since.

Chapter 15
THE DEBUTANTE MURDERER

Suzanne Clift

*J*ohn Anzalone was like any other cab driver looking for his next fare at South Station on the evening of October 4, 1962. A fine-looking young woman approached the cab. She was dressed very fashionably in a high-necked blue shantung dress, carrying a small suitcase with her dachshund in tow. She requested a ride to 85 Pinckney Street in Beacon Hill. Perfect, thought Anzalone. A short trip from a rich girl—the tip should be big, and the trip will be quick. The more rides to Beacon Hill, the better.

But it didn't quite work out that way. After they arrived in Beacon Hill, the girl changed her mind. Instead, she wanted to go to the Statler Hilton Hotel (now the Park Plaza Hotel). Sure thing, he thought. Longer trip, bigger tip. Arriving in the Back Bay, the young woman quickly got out, told him to take care of the dog and promptly jumped into another cab. In a flash, she was gone. Anzalone dismissed this behavior; the rich sometimes pulled stunts like this. But something didn't click. The girl's erratic behavior, and the fact that he'd gotten a dog in the bargain, made him think he'd better report this one to the police. Good thing, too—she may have seemed a little flighty to him, but there was a manhunt going on to track down this woman. She wasn't a clueless airhead. She was wanted for murder.

THE DEBUTANTE

Suzanne Clift was from one of Boston's elite families, growing up with the crème de la crème in Beacon Hill. She was raised as many of her peers were—with the best of the best. She went to a private Boston finishing school, spoke fluent French, sailed, studied ballet and later attended Mount Holyoke College. She had the added élan of being the niece of handsome Hollywood star of the previous decade Montgomery Clift.

After she left her studies as a sophomore at Mount Holyoke, Suzanne took up residence with her grandmother at her home at 85 Pinckney Street in Beacon Hill.

Suzanne was shy and hadn't dated much. Then, in 1960, she met a handsome Italian named Piero Brentani on a blind date. For almost two years the two courted, and she fell head over heels in love with him. It's unclear how Brentani felt about her; even her stepfather admitted, "I know Suzanne was deeply in love with Piero. As for Piero, well, how can you tell when a man is deeply in love?" Although Piero was said to be something of a ladies' man, he was a catch—tall, dark and handsome. He was born into an equally well-to-do Italian family and raised all over Europe and South America.

Brentani moved to Boston to attend the Massachusetts Institute of Technology for an advanced degree. Once he had his diploma in hand, he decided that it was time to leave Boston for a job on the West Coast, after a long vacation back in Italy. The two spent their final two weeks together in Suzanne's home while her grandmother was taking a short vacation on Cape Cod. On the night he told her that he was leaving, the two acted like nothing had changed. They went to bed and listened to the opera *Don Giovanni* on the radio. Ironically enough, the opera is about Don Juan, the famous philanderer who left a long list of broken hearts. Perhaps it was the passion of the music or the realization that she was dating a real Don Juan that drove Suzanne to take a gun to bed with her. It might have been to kill herself. But it was Brentani who ended up dead.

THE MURDER

In the tiny bedroom that night, Suzanne couldn't sleep. She took the gun from beneath her pillow and contemplated the thirteen-inch barrel placed against her own temple for hours in the darkness. She awoke, suddenly shocked out of her stupor. The gun had gone off—she didn't know how—and Brentani was dead. Shot in the back of the head as he lay sleeping.

It wasn't until a day later that Suzanne went on the move. She booked a flight to Rio de Janeiro with her little dog, Schnipsi. She spent the hours-long flight getting there only to turn around and come right back. That's when she hailed Anzalone's cab.

In the meantime, Suzanne's grandmother, Barbara Pierce Pearmain, came back from her summer home in Osterville, Cape Cod. Imagine her surprise at finding the door to Suzanne's upstairs

The scene of the crime: 85 Pinckney Street in Beacon Hill. *Photo by Dina Vargo.*

bedroom padlocked, no Suzanne and a .22-caliber gun in the kitchen. The gun, it was found later, had been reported stolen from a Philadelphia home where Suzanne had stayed the previous summer.

Suzanne's grandmother was able to break down the bedroom door and discovered, under a sheet, the naked and bloody body of Brentani and a short note from Suzanne, giving away all that she owned. Suzanne's grandmother immediately called the police, and an international manhunt for the debutante was on.

Once Suzanne had arrived back in Boston, she requested the second cab she hopped into to take her to nearby Massachusetts General Hospital for psychiatric care. She entered the emergency ward, sat on a bench and cried. The police were called, and she immediately confessed to the murder. She offered no explanation.

Perhaps there was an explanation. Suzanne was pregnant with Brentani's baby.

THE TRIAL

At her court date, over two hundred spectators watched as she stood silent when the judge asked for her plea. The judge presiding over her case permitted a lesser charge of manslaughter after a three-day hearing proved that Suzanne had been diagnosed with schizophrenia. Her defense lawyers presented her case. They said she suffered from a lack of a caring and loving family. She spoke at her trial in February 1963, telling the judge about her troubled personal life. She'd received psychiatric treatment countless times and spent years struggling with depression and suicidal thoughts. All this came to a head when Brentani refused to marry her. She claimed that she kept her pregnancy a secret. "I knew his feelings. He had told me if I ever became pregnant, I would have to have an abortion." She was stuck.

THE SENTENCE

On February 12, 1963, Suzanne was found guilty of manslaughter. She was sentenced to ten years of probation on the condition that she commit herself to the Massachusetts Mental Health Center for treatment. Experts thought it was possible that she could be cured of her personality disorder in three to five years. By all accounts, Suzanne was relieved; she wanted the chance to be with her baby after its birth. She got her wish. Suzanne gave birth to a healthy baby girl on June 3, 1963, at the Boston Lying-In Hospital, today a part of Brigham and Women's Hospital.

Chapter 16
THE SPICE OF LIFE

Julia Child

S he felt like a failure. She had just been fired from a job where she was in over her head. She had a fanciful, but at the same time unshakable, belief that she was destined for something greater. But what?

She was almost thirty years old. She'd tried her hand at writing advertising copy in New York City, but it didn't fulfill her. She managed marketing in a retail store, but that just wasn't her calling. She wrote a fashion column, which she found "loathsome." She wanted to travel the world. She wanted to write. She wanted romance. But all she'd done so far was fail at finding meaningful employment and, even worse, fail at finding love.

She was skilled at being a socialite—making the rounds of her friends' and parents' friends' homes in conservative and comfortable Pasadena. But where was the meaning in all that? Where was the adventure? Where was the *life*? As America entered World War II in 1941, she knew what she had to do: enlist. Opportunities for a woman her age may have been limited, but certainly the United States government could use her help.

Who knew that this one decision would change her life forever? She really would travel the world. She'd become a bestselling author. She'd even break bread with the Mafiosi. She'd do it all while turning the new medium of television on its head, becoming an early reality-television star. Maybe she'd even become...a spy? Julia Child was truly destined to experience the spice of life.

BLAND BEGINNINGS

Julia McWilliams was born in Pasadena, California, on August 15, 1912, to an affluent family. An active girl with a touch of a wild side, she rode her bicycle all over Pasadena and played pranks on her younger siblings. She was popular and social, eventually attending her mother's top-tier alma mater back east, Smith College in western Massachusetts. After graduation, the romantic young lady went off to New York City to find her fortune. She fancied herself an important writer but was rejected by both *Newsweek* and the *New Yorker* magazines. She didn't get much traction writing for any other publications but did land a position writing advertising copy for a furniture store called W.&J. Sloane's in New York City. It would have to do. After falling for the wrong guy and suffering a broken heart, she returned to Pasadena to lick her wounds and wonder about her future.

In California, she found comfort in being a social butterfly. She spent time flitting about from party to party. She also volunteered for the Junior League and other similar organizations while being courted by a very eligible and rich newspaper owner. Much to her father's displeasure, Julia rejected the man's advances because she wasn't in love with him. Although she knew that her options were narrowing with age, she was a romantic to the core and just couldn't bring herself to settle. She also saw her career options diminishing, so when she was offered a position at the Beverly Hills W.&J. Sloane store as the advertising manager, she took it. She faked it to make it and readily admitted that she didn't have the business acumen to be successful in this job. She held it together for a while, handling a substantial budget, a small staff and the responsibility for all the marketing and advertising for the store. Her eyes were bigger than her stomach, though, and it caught up to her. She was fired for insubordination, of all things. That shake-up left her more determined to get serious about her future. With an appetite for more, she set out to find the right fit for her.

YOU'RE IN THE SERVICE NOW

As Julia began to mull over her future, the United States officially entered World War II. This was the chance she was looking for. She moved to Washington, D.C., and applied to become either a WAVE (the women's division of the U.S. Navy) or a WAC (Women's Army Corps). But neither the WAVEs nor the WACs would have her because of her height. At six feet and two inches, she was deemed too tall. C'est la vie!

She was tickled when her luck changed and she was accepted to work at the Office of Strategic Services (OSS), an early precursor to the CIA. It ran a network of spies and military intelligence across the world. Would this be her opportunity to become a spy? To see the world? To make a difference? Well, not yet. She was stuck in the D.C. office doing mind-numbing administrative work. Occasionally, she was posted on some interesting projects, like helping researchers develop shark repellant that would be used on missiles to ensure that sharks didn't set them off prematurely if they encountered them in the deep. But the truth is, it was a slog.

That is, it was, until the OSS announced it would be expanding its operations to Asia. Julia immediately signed on. It wasn't too tall an order. Julia would finally be a world traveler. She was sent to Ceylon and fell in love—with her exotic surroundings, her intellectual colleagues, her work and a man. But the relationship would take a little time to simmer before coming to a boil. In the meantime, Julia had a job to do. This entailed setting up and managing the Southeast Asia Command post of the OSS, which was largely administrative. Was she a spy? Probably not. But she did have to have a high level of clearance to handle the classified documents and orders that she organized.

It wasn't until she was transferred to Kunming, China, that she started to get to know a man she'd met in Ceylon named Paul Child. Initially taken in by her long legs, Paul wasn't immediately interested, though they spent time together having dinners and talking. The two became close, but the relationship was one-sided until the day that Paul woke up and smelled the coffee. When the war was coming to a close and the two were discussing their unsettled futures, Paul had an epiphany. He really had a thing for this fun-loving, try-anything-once woman. They started a long-distance relationship when they arrived back in the States, spent a few weeks traveling the country together and got hitched in 1946. They settled in Washington, D.C., as Paul continued to work for the government and Julia became a homemaker. That is, until his auspicious transfer to France. Life would never be the same.

Viva la France

Julia was overjoyed to be moving to Paris. Not just France, but Paris. It was a dream come true. And the food was truly life-changing. She wrote longingly of her most memorable meal in letters and again later in life in her memoirs. It was sole meunière—a classic dish of white fish served in a browned butter and lemon sauce. How could something so simple be so good? It was like nothing she'd ever had before. This was worth more exploration!

She wasn't a born cook. In fact, she was historically clumsy in the kitchen. She had cooked a few times with her sister-in-law back in the States, but the food in France demanded further study. She started in the markets that were, again, a wholly different experience than in the States. She tried everything. She drank wine that was, again, not nearly as available in the States then as it is today. She talked with neighborhood grocers and butchers and cheesemongers. She was a ravenous student.

As Julia and Paul settled into their new life, Julia again thought about what she was going to do with her life. And now, at thirty-six, without a job, she cast about for a meaningful way to spend her days. What could she do? What could she become? She liked to eat; that much she knew. What if she could cook in the French style? Could she really understand and master French cooking? Soon enough, she was enrolled at Le Cordon Bleu. She became a star pupil, practicing the day's lessons between classes in the afternoon and evening.

As she studied, she became exacting, a perfectionist. She wanted to explore every recipe inside and out, to develop an understanding of every nuance. It was an art and a science that demanded trial runs, small adjustments and constant experimentation. She was in her element. All the data that she was collecting would be necessary for her next leap in the years to come—writing a cookbook.

Sole Mates

Enter Simone Beck, or simply Simca, as friends called her. Simca was a woman of Julia's own heart. She was equally obsessed with cooking but on a more personal level, exploring her family's traditional recipes. She and another friend, Louisette Bertholle, were delving into the recipes they'd both grown up with in France. Julia ate it up. The three women called themselves the Trois Gourmandes. They met to cook, share techniques and recipes and, eventually, to open a small cooking school to teach other women how to cook. At that time, despite cooking and kitchen life being a traditional women's "place," any real credibility around cooking was still owned by men, who, as ever, kept women out of their exclusive club.

Meanwhile, Simca and Louisette had a side project: writing up their recipes for a cookbook. They intended to teach American women how to cook the French way. They'd found their missing ingredient. It was Julia. They had an American publisher on board, and all they thought they needed was help with translation. Julia did more than that; she revolutionized the way cookbooks were written. She introduced a familiar, helpful voice in her writing. She clarified recipes using precise measurements and clear instructions. She knew they had something special to offer. Now they just needed the right publisher. Enter Avis.

Avis DeSoto lived in Cambridge, Massachusetts, and had contacts in the publishing world. Julia and Avis became friends over mail after Julia wrote a letter to Avis's husband, who had written an article bemoaning the lack of quality knives available in America. Nothing brings people together like cutlery! Avis responded to Julia, and a friendship was sealed. They sent each other photos and long letters for years before meeting face to face. As luck would have it, Avis became a champion for the book stateside. Simca and Julia plowed through hundreds of tastings and testings of recipes. The process took years of work. This was no slapdash affair. If anything was worth doing, it was worth doing right. All the while, Julia and Paul were transferred from Paris to Marseille to Bonn, back to D.C. and then to Oslo. The whole time, Julia explored the local cuisine, learned what she could and kept working on the book.

When *Mastering the Art of French Cooking* finally came out in 1961, the American book-buying market was a tough nut to crack. At that time in America, everything was focused on using the time-saving measures and new technologies the Atomic Age had to offer. Frozen TV dinners were the latest rage. Canned vegetables were the norm—all the better to take to that new bomb shelter in the backyard. Who was the audience? How would they be convinced that spending some quality time in the kitchen would produce quality food? All Americans needed to hear was the wobbly, high-pitched voice of Julia Child.

TV DINNER

Julia and Paul moved to Cambridge when they decided to stay in the States for good after Paul retired. Avis lived in the neighborhood. It was close to both some of Julia's and Paul's family members. And the community offered the diverse and intellectual mix of people that the two were accustomed to socializing with during their years abroad. They became Cantabrigians. Their home at 103 Irving Street was soon outfitted with what was to become the best-known kitchen in all of American history.

To sell the book, Julia was invited to appear as a guest on the local Boston PBS affiliate, WGBH, in 1962. Instead of doing the expected static interview, she turned the opportunity on its head. Why just sit and chat about the book when cooking was best explained by demonstration? She would teach viewers how to make a simple but delicious recipe from the book: an omelet. The brass at WGBH wasn't sure what to expect, but they made preparations in a makeshift kitchen and hoped that the show wasn't a

Julia Child brandishes a mallet on the set of one of her earliest shows with WGBH. Note her shirt with the "Ecole Tres Gourmandes" patch. *Courtesy of the Trustees of the Boston Public Library.*

recipe for disaster. Their risk paid off. People loved it. Julia, all six feet, two inches of her, complete with wobbly voice, was a natural. Her strength was her personality, her confidence, her warmth, not to mention her knowledge, which she communicated with ease. WGBH got so many letters and calls that Julia was given her own show, *The French Chef*. During her long time on-air, she refused to apologize for mistakes, tossing knives over her shoulder cavalierly. She rolled with the punches. All of this served her well and helped her to become a household name.

American women were starved for a personality like Julia's, and they were starved for the information she was sharing: good food, simply made with fresh ingredients and butter—lots and lots of butter. She directly addressed her viewers, and she did so with no pretension. Not merely a star, but a legend, was born.

From her debut in 1962 to her last show in 2000, she took part in thirteen television series. She wrote or co-wrote seventeen cookbooks and one memoir. She revolutionized cooking in the United States. She mentored and promoted American chefs, many of whom she found in Boston. She was willing to change with the times—except when it came to anything smelling like a diet. She'd never give up butter or salt. "The only time to eat diet food is while you're waiting for the steak to cook," she said.

SPICE OF LIFE

Julia was a spicy one long before she became famous. She was a committed Democrat who was deeply troubled by the witch hunts for Communists (real or imagined) carried out by followers of Senator Joseph McCarthy in the 1950s. Since joining the armed forces, she socialized mostly with intellectuals, some of whom had far left-leaning beliefs. Indeed, some of her friends and associates were called up and questioned by the House Un-American Activities Committee. This cut extremely close to home when her husband was questioned in 1955. He was questioned for weeks. When it came to light that some suspected him of being homosexual, he and Julia had a good laugh. This prompted a most public and cheeky response. For their annual Valentine's Day card, the two posed naked, covered only by the bubbles in a cozy-looking bath, flutes of champagne at the ready.

Julia could also take a serious stand when one was called for. During the McCarthy era, people accused others of being associated with Communism on the basis of the most innocuous activities, with or without proof. In 1954, before her husband was accused, Julia was incensed when a woman charged five members of the Smith College faculty of Communist leanings. This woman also implied that they weren't the only ones, that others at the school were hiding in the shadows, and until they were rooted out, alumni might want to reconsider making any donations to the school. When Julia got wind of these baseless accusations, she wrote an open letter to the school and all its alumni, calling out the accuser for her irresponsibility in having absolutely no credible evidence to make such a claim publicly. Julia took a stand for "proper democratic methods" and against "totalitarian" approaches while doubling her annual contribution to the school.

Julia also knew how to have a good time with people from all walks of life. If fun, food and drink were on tap, Julia was game. She wouldn't even let the Mafia get in the way of that. Author Bob Spitz recounts a story in his book, *Dearie*, about a meal Julia had in a restaurant in Boston's North End. One evening Julia was having dinner at Jasper White's restaurant. The traditionally Italian neighborhood of Boston had more than its fair share of residents on the "family" payroll. When two men who were well-known criminals came in expecting the best seat in the house, Chef White very nervously told them that it had been taken by Julia. Rather than being upset, the two Mafiosi acted like smitten schoolgirls. They insisted on buying Julia a very expensive bottle of champagne. Chef White checked in with Julia to see if she would accept it, and of course she would! The hardboiled dons approached Julia's dinner party, and the group talked for a time about—what else?—good food.

JUST DESSERTS

In 2001, Julia decided to retire to Santa Barbara. Upon leaving her Cambridge home, where she'd lived for forty years and taped three television series, she agreed to donate her kitchen to the Smithsonian Institution's National Museum of American History in Washington, D.C. In the same building that holds such quintessential pieces of American history as the Star-Spangled Banner, Dorothy's ruby slippers and the first light bulb created by Thomas Edison, viewers can walk around Julia's kitchen, which looks so comfortable and inviting that you can practically smell the omelet sizzling in the pan. Taken piece by piece from her home and reconstructed in the museum, Julia's kitchen is one of the most popular displays in the permanent collection.

In August 2004, Julia Child, the first woman ever inducted into the Culinary Institute Hall of Fame and winner of France's Legion d'Honneur, died in California, just two days shy of her ninety-second birthday. For someone who at one time wasn't sure where her fortunes lay, she managed to blaze a path for women and for chefs, television networks and reality stars. She embarked on a journey to find meaning in her own life and created meaning in the lives of many, doing it all with more than a pinch of zest.

Chapter 17

RUNNING WILD

Kathrine Switzer

*L*ike many April days in Boston, this one was wet and raw, with alternating snow and raindrops splashing the pavement. The group of four made their way to the race start, covered up in sweatpants and shirts, with hoods up, to retain their warmth for as long as possible. They joined the other 730 runners and nervously awaited the start. Occasionally, another runner would look over and notice a little something different about the runner all in gray who was a little smaller than the others. On second glance, was that a girl? How could that be? This was the 1967 Boston Marathon, after all. Were women even allowed to run it? And she had a numbered bib—#261. Most of the runners who noticed were taken aback but friendly to her, especially when her proud coach patted her on the back and bragged to anyone who'd listen that she was a great runner and she'd go all the way. Her friend and boyfriend nodded appreciatively.

She, on the other hand, played it low-key. She was here to run, not to protest, and certainly she had no thought of starting a movement. Not that that stopped her from wearing lipstick. And anyway, she had no idea that women weren't permitted to run the Boston Marathon. Her coach, Arnie, had checked it all out. She registered just like anyone else, signing her name K.V. Switzer, using her initials just like the authors she admired. She paid and sent in a waiver from her university's doctor saying that she was fit to run. Everything was on the up-and-up, and she was thrilled to get started. Nothing was going to stop her from participating in the first and longest-running marathon in the United States. She'd been training for

Jock Semple, Boston Marathon co-director, runs alongside Kathrine Switzer (#261), trying to grab her number. Kathrine's boyfriend Tom (#390) has just cross-blocked Jock. *Courtesy of the Trustees of the Boston Public Library.*

months and had even run a full thirty-one miles with her coach as a trial run. She was ready. The rest of the world was another question.

Not far into the run, a press truck filled with writers and photographers was motoring alongside them, on its way to cover the front runners. As it passed, the runners around her all waved and smiled. This was their smile-for-the-camera moment. Then, she noticed the press truck slow down and the media folks start to point at her. She became the focus of their attention. Little did they all know that the photographs about to be taken would be shown around the world later that day and become a symbol for the women's movement for years to come. Kathrine Switzer was about to be chased down and physically accosted by the race director. Her life was about to change forever.

Beginnings

Kathrine Switzer (yep, that's the spelling; her father, in a mad rush in the delivery room, misspelled what was likely intended to be Katherine) was born on January 5, 1947, in Amberg, Germany, into a military family. She grew up in Virginia. In an effort to interest her in a sport other than cheerleading, her father suggested she take up track and field. He insisted that she shouldn't be on the sidelines cheering for others; she should be the one the crowd was cheering for. She bought the idea and started to run in high school. She loved it, even if her friends weren't so sure. They thought she might develop big thighs and grow a mustache. But she kept at it, and it made her feel so strong, so good and confident that she called it her "secret weapon."

There weren't many options for women to participate in sports in college. She transferred to Syracuse University in 1966 and agreed to train with the track team, even though she couldn't participate in meets. The guys were nice enough, and she struck up a friendship with an older coach named Arnie Briggs, who seemed to be excited to run, and talk to, just about anyone. Even a girl! They formed a fast friendship as they ran miles and miles together over the frozen tundra of upstate New York, and he would talk incessantly about the Boston Marathon. A former marathon runner, he would mythologize the marathon and tell her about the races, the personalities, the records broken and the spirits broken on Heartbreak Hill. As she explains in her memoir, at one point she got so tired of him talking about it, she exclaimed, "Oh Arnie, let's quit talking about the Boston Marathon and run the damn thing!" He was surprised and explained to her that that just wasn't possible; women couldn't run that long a distance. Kathrine had heard that another woman, Roberta Bingay (later Gibb), had, in fact, run it earlier that year, but he didn't believe her. They argued, but when pressed, Arnie conceded that if any woman could run the Boston Marathon, it would be Kathrine. They struck a deal, and training began.

1967 Boston Marathon

After those many months of long runs during the winter in Syracuse, culminating in a thirty-one-mile run, it wouldn't all go to waste because of some close-minded Neanderthal type. Just as the press truck passed, an imposing man came out of nowhere and took Kathrine's breath away, screaming, "Get the hell out of my race and give me those numbers!" Jock Semple, the race co-director, was incensed. No woman was going to turn his race into some bra-burning circus, and no one was going to make a fool of him. He chased her down, grasping for her numbers. In shock, as anyone would be, Kathrine was able to keep her wits about her and stay the course. Her boyfriend, a brawny guy, took a running leap at Jock and knocked him to the side of the road. She felt awful about that but just kept running. Then it got very, very quiet.

For miles and miles, she replayed the scene over in her head. She finally told Arnie, "I don't know about you, but I have to finish this." He agreed. She knew that now this was more than just a race. This was more than just a personal accomplishment. If she didn't finish, she'd prove to everyone that women couldn't run long distances—that they were indeed the weaker sex. She was determined to finish, even if she had to do it on her hands and knees. Luckily, it didn't come to that. She came in at a respectable four hours and twenty minutes. And she finished knowing what she was going to do for the rest of her life.

As she says in the documentary *Makers*, she was angry. Angry that other women weren't running in the marathon. She was angry that the longest track event for women in the Olympics was the eight-hundred-meter race. She realized that there was no such thing as a sports scholarship for women, and not very many college sports teams included women. And she realized that it was not because women weren't interested. It was that too few opportunities existed for women to get involved. She set her mind on her trip home to Syracuse to change that. And she vowed to return to Boston the next year and improve her time.

In the meantime, there were headlines and hate mail. The *New York Times* declared, "Lady with Desire to Run Crashed Marathon." It went further, declaring that "officials at Boston shaken when entry 261 started race." Wow! If the officials were shaken, how would they imagine Kathrine felt after she was attacked on the course? The article went on to state that she "supposedly finished" the run of twenty-six miles and 385 yards, and the writers stood by the race officials, who were, after all, just doing their job, enforcing the rules. Race co-director Will Cloney was quoted as saying, "Women can't run in the marathon because the rules forbid it...We have no place in the marathon for any unauthorized person, even a man. If that girl were my daughter, I would spank her."

Another rule-breaker, Roberta Gibb, did run and finish, but without a bib number, her entry was deemed "unofficial." She was easy for the race organizers to ignore. Kathrine wasn't.

As an added insult to her experience, a quick twenty-four hours after the marathon, she received a letter by express delivery expelling her from the Amateur Athletic Union (AAU) for (1) fraudulently running the race, (2) running more than a mile and a half, (3) running with men and (4) running without a chaperone.

MARATHON WOMAN

Kathrine set out to prove a great deal, and with years of tireless work, she did it over and over again. Personally, she felt that, in order for women to be taken more seriously as runners, she herself would need to improve. Because she was one of only a handful of female runners, she believed that it was incumbent on her to transform herself from a "jogger" into an elite runner. With the kind of training only runners understand, including one-hundred-mile weeks, interval training and more blisters than anyone can imagine, she made that transformation. Her best running time was a 2:51:37 in the 1975 Boston Marathon, when she placed second, and her biggest victory came in 1974 in the New York City Marathon, coming in first place among the women. This was her thirty-second marathon, meaning she had run more than four marathons per year since 1967. And she did it all while working a full-time job and volunteering a lot of time getting races for female runners organized and off the ground.

She accomplished all this without the specialized running attire we take for granted today, which may seem inconsequential but definitely impacted her time. Running shorts were not made for the shape of a woman's body, so Kathrine ran, instead, in tennis dresses. This got her in a bit of trouble with the more radical adherents of the women's movement who thought she should dress more like a man, be less feminine and not sell out to "the Establishment." However, the tennis dress made good running sense because men's shorts and tops chafed so badly. She says in the documentary *Makers* that she was "damned if she did and damned if she didn't." Running shoes were also not made for women and, in fact, were not readily available even for men. She ordered the smallest men's sizes from Europe and suffered the consequences, with blisters so bad she'd finish every marathon with bloodied feet.

Because of Kathrine's work, by 1972, women could run officially in the Boston Marathon by meeting the qualifying time of 3:30. With a small cadre of other female runners, Kathrine ran all over the world as they worked to promote women's running. She helped organize the first women-only "mini-marathon" in New York City. Starting in 1972 with seventy-eight runners, the popular 10K race continues today with over five thousand finishers. She was instrumental in bringing key sponsorships to running events, like connecting Olympic Airlines to the New York City Marathon in its earliest days.

All of her successes culminated in the achievement of her greatest goal: the acceptance of the women's marathon at the Olympic Games. That was no small undertaking, and it took years of building ground to come to fruition. In 1978, she began by launching the Avon Running Circuit for women. This was a series of marathons that hopped around the world—Los Angeles, Tokyo, Rio de Janeiro, Paris, Moscow and London—eventually growing to four hundred races in twenty-seven countries for over one million women. The series served to convince the Olympic Games organizers that the marathon was not only a serious women's sport but a popular one at that. The number of participants increased with each race, and the caliber of the competitors rose, as well. In February 1981, it was official—the first women's marathon would be held during the Los Angeles Olympic Games in 1984.

You've Run a Long Way, Baby

Kathrine's impact on the running world has been tremendous. Running USA, a nonprofit organization created to improve the status of road racing in the United States, annually releases a Marathon Report, tracking the number of marathon finishers by gender and age. It has found that since 1990, the number of marathon finishers in the United States has increased more than 140 percent and the number of female finishers has increased from 10 percent of all finishers in 1980 to 43 percent in 2013. It is breathtaking to think that only one woman officially ran a marathon in America not that long ago.

For all that Kathrine accomplished, she was named Female Runner of the Decade by *Runner's World* magazine in 1977 and later inducted into the National

Portrait of marathon woman Kathrine Switzer, taken in May 2011, in the apple orchards near her American home in the Hudson Valley of New York State. *Photo by Joan Barker Images and courtesy of Kathrine Switzer's website.*

Women's Hall of Fame in 2011. She's won an Emmy for her work on television and can be found supporting causes near to her heart by serving as a speaker at various conferences around the world. She comes back to the Boston Marathon every year, where she sits on multiple expert panels prior to the race and serves as a commentator during the race.

Her work is not yet done. She has recognized that while America has come a long way in making opportunities available for women to participate in sports, the same is not true around the world. While in the United States women make up a full 60 percent of the field in half marathons, in Spain, they represent only 13 to 18 percent. If anyone can help change that, it's Kathrine, who's started 261 Fearless, a network of women's running clubs across the world. She kicked the effort off with a women's-only marathon and 10K in Mallorca, Spain, in March 2014. Still the only women's-only marathon in all of Europe, 700 runners participated in the 2014 edition, and 3,500 are expected to run in 2015.

The woman who set out to run a marathon in 1967 to prove to herself that she could has managed to realize that, and so much more.

Chapter 18

GUIDING LIGHT

Sally Snowman

On a small grassy island eight miles out in the Boston Harbor, a small group of people gathered. Despite the island being populated since 1716, they'd be witnessing something that had never happened there in 278 years. Welcomed by a warm breeze and an inviting sunny blue sky, twenty people disembarked from a random assortment of boats and watercraft. They were dressed casually, drinking in the scenery, aware that they were taking part in a special ritual. The guests of honor arrived on a thirty-two-foot vessel appropriately called the *True Love*. They were greeted by their family and friends and by another old island companion—the Boston Light.

Standing since 1783 (the original structure built in 1716 was destroyed during the Revolutionary War), the Boston Light has looked out over Boston's harbor, sending out its guiding rays to soldiers and sailors and even airmen. It's served as a protector, as a guide, as a symbol of hope to those searching for land. On this calm day in October 1994, it was standing sentry while two people took a vow of love. The first wedding ever performed on Little Brewster Island was taking place. It was a dream come true for Sally Snowman, who'd known since she first visited the island when she was ten years old that she wanted to be married there. Incredibly, she would also become the first female lighthouse keeper in the history of the United States Coast Guard.

Jill of All Trades

Sally Snowman grew up in Weymouth, Massachusetts, a town on Boston's south shore, where the ocean and beaches were always part of her life. She went to Bridgewater State College (now University) and started a teaching career. While her degree centered on elementary education, she was able to minor in both music and outdoor education, then a new field of study. She worked primarily in the Weymouth Public Schools teaching kindergarten through eighth grade, but she was also employed seasonally at the Thompson Island Education Center in Boston Harbor, putting that outdoor education minor to use.

In the mid-1980s, Sally went through a period of reevaluation and decided to reset her career. She wound up taking a break from teaching for a bit and worked as a temporary office employee in a hospital pharmacy. While it was extremely uncommon for the hospital administrators to ever hire from the temp agency, they liked Sally's work and brought her on full time. Within the first year of her employment there, Sally decided to go back to school for a master's degree in education at Curry College. Coincidentally at the same time, the hospital began thinking about establishing a twenty-four-hour day-care center for its employees' children. It was a combination of Sally's experience as an educator and her decision to make early education the focus of her thesis that placed her on the hospital's research committee to determine the feasibility of establishing the day-care center. While the hospital moved ahead with providing the day-care center, she stayed on in an administrative capacity as she continued her classwork.

Another event would soon play a major role in developing her professional life: she was diagnosed, at thirty years old, with a learning disability, attention deficit disorder (ADD). While being diagnosed with a learning disability may not seem auspicious, gifts are often disguised as problems. As she worked in administration for the hospital, Curry College hired her on a part-time basis to teach new students study and life skills—the same set of skills she'd developed in her own life.

After she graduated, she joined the faculty of Curry College, where she remained until 2004. During her tenure, she also opened the Snowman Learning Center as a way to continue teaching life and study skills to adults and children with learning disabilities. She became an expert in the field, writing two books that addressed ADD in adults: *Rising to the Challenge: Understanding Adults with ADD and Other Learning Difficulties* and the *Rising to the Challenge Workbook*. This work took her around the country giving lectures and workshops. But her home was always near the sea.

SEMPER PARATUS

The United States Coast Guard has been in existence since 1790 as a branch of the United States Armed Forces. Its main mission is maritime law enforcement as a department of Homeland Security, but it's traditionally known for taking care of stranded ships and performing search and rescue operations. What is less known is that it plays a role in protecting the maritime environment, which encompasses everything from stopping pollution to helping whales get back to sea to responding to environmental crises like oil spills and hurricane damage. Its work is best summed up in the words of Admiral Robert J. Papp Jr., the twenty-fourth commandant of the U.S. Coast Guard: "We protect those on the Sea. We protect America from threats delivered by Sea, and we protect the Sea itself." It also maintains what are called "aids to navigation"—in other words, lighthouses.

The U.S. Coast Guard also retains a large auxiliary contingent. The Coast Guard Auxiliary is a force of civilian volunteers who assist the Coast Guard in achieving its mission. As of 2012, there were 32,156 active auxiliarists across the United States. Their focus is mainly boater safety and education, but in Boston, their role has been expanded to provide a presence on the Boston Harbor Islands and, in particular, at the Boston Light.

Sally joined the auxiliary in 1976 at the age of twenty-four, following in the footsteps of her father, Roger Snowman. (She didn't know how closely she was following those footsteps. As it turned out, he had joined in 1949, also at the age of twenty-four. She didn't make that connection until many years later at his fiftieth anniversary recognition ceremony.) Her father played a leadership role in the auxiliary, serving as district commodore and developing both an Operations Department and a Communications Department on the national level.

Sally was looking for something different to do other than teaching school and working to pay her tuition. She worked with her father performing safety patrols on her family's boat during the summer months and on weekends. She helped teach boating classes during the off-season, but her real passion was in developing larger programs for the public. She had started volunteering at the Boston Light in the early 1990s. After Little Brewster Island became a part of the Boston Harbor Island National Recreation Area in 1989, there was a need for interpretive programming, and the perfect person stepped into the void: Sally.

The Boston Light

The Boston Light was the first lighthouse built in the United States, though it's the second oldest lighthouse structure still in existence (the oldest was built in 1764 in Sandy Hook, New Jersey). The light was ceded from Massachusetts to the new United States government in 1790. From then on, it was operated by a series of male lighthouse keepers who both maintained the island and took care of and operated the light. Lighthouse keepers traditionally stayed on the island with their families and pets. Many a story has been handed down about the keepers and the goings-on at the island, like George Worthylake, the first keeper, whose family was drowned when their boat capsized as they were returning to the island from Boston. That tragic story is so well known because Benjamin Franklin published a ballad about it. There's also the story of the "Cuban" cigar factory that was set up on the island to sell fraudulent cigars to Bostonians. That keeper didn't "keep" his job for long. There are stories of heroes and tragedies fit for one of America's most historic places. The next chapter for the light, though, had more to do with preserving history and making some new history.

In the 1920s, the U.S. Coast Guard started to automate lighthouses. By 1989, a plan was in place to automate the Boston Light. Preservationists

A postcard printed by Tichnor Bros. Inc. of Boston showing the Boston Light in Boston Harbor, circa 1930–1945. The large building in the center no longer exists. *Courtesy of the Trustees of the Boston Public Library.*

put up a fight, arguing that the light could easily be vandalized without the protection of a full-time keeper. A figure with as much celebrity as the light itself took up the mantle of protecting it; Massachusetts senator Edward M. Kennedy sponsored an amendment to previous legislation to keep the lighthouse permanently manned. It is now the only lighthouse still owned by the U.S. Coast Guard with a paid full-time keeper. However, the light is no longer manned; it's "womanned."

SHE SAW THE LIGHT

Sally points out that until she married her husband, fellow auxiliarist and Boston Light volunteer Jay Thomson, she would not have been able to stay at the light alone or as a guest not married to the keeper, out of traditional decorum and propriety. Now, she is the keeper.

Although it certainly didn't happen overnight, she and the island are a natural fit. She started to volunteer at the Boston Light in 1994, giving tours and developing a curriculum for schoolchildren that could be used as a guide for visiting tourists. Additionally, she and her husband studied the island to produce a comprehensive history, compiled in their book, *Boston Light: A Historical Perspective*. In 1999, when the book was published, the management and future of the Boston Light was unclear. Since that time, the light has been automated, and the island is managed by a three-way partnership: the island is part of the Boston Harbor Islands National Park (BHINP), the light is still under the aegis of the U.S. Coast Guard and Boston Harbor Islands Alliance serves as the fundraising arm that acts on behalf of the national park, which is not permitted to raise funds for itself. Another, no less important, group that also plays a role at the island is the Friends of the Boston Harbor Islands (FBHI). This is a private nonprofit that provides volunteers to the island (as well as the other islands in the national park) as historical interpreters.

While the job of lighthouse keeper may no longer entail hours of cleaning the brasswork (refer to her book to read an epic poem written by a previous keeper on that undesirable duty), since 2003, Sally has served as site supervisor and safety officer. She oversees the physical maintenance of not just the lighthouse but all the buildings associated with the site; she recruits and trains new volunteers; she serves as a liaison between the managing partners of the Boston Harbor Islands; she is the light historian; and she also deals with the media. Her next big outreach project will be coordinating events celebrating the 300th anniversary of the building of the original Boston Light. To make her job resonate more with both herself and tourists, she dons the clothes typical for a woman in the early nineteenth century.

Sally is very humble when discussing how she got the job as the first-ever female U.S. Coast Guard lighthouse keeper in the history of the United States. She says that she simply applied for it. While that may be true, she was also the perfect person for it. It seems like the road rose up to meet her; she had the perfect combination of skills, temperament, passion for the job and the environment, as well as a history of serving in the Coast Guard.

She's always loved the island. Ever since her father took her there as a ten-year-old, it has been a magical and transformative place for her. While she's perfectly suited to take on the day-to-day administrative tasks and the teaching and she is able to work within what some may see as a strict government structure, Sally has another side. That side is tuned in to the natural rhythms of the ocean, sea and sky. She appreciates those moments of quietude and absorbs the full experience of living with the light—a place where nights are peaceful, with only the clanking of the bell buoy in the ocean and calling of seagulls overhead. She's never surprised when tourists come with a picnic and lose all track of time. That's Sally's other goal—to get people to have a moment, live in peace and take that back to the city with them. She says, "Every cell in their body can remember this experience. They just have to call upon it."

BIBLIOGRAPHY

Adams, Dan. "Ceremony Honors Cyclist Who Broke Barriers." *Boston Globe*, September 30, 2013.

Aronson, Sidney H. "The Sociology of the Bicycle." *Social Forces* 30, no. 3 (March 1952).

Baker, Julie. "The Troubled Voyage of *Neptune's Car*." *American History* (February 2005).

Beam, Alex. "Mrs. Gardner's Annual Claim on Heaven." *Boston Globe*, April 19, 1995, 57.

Berkin, Carol. *Revolutionary Mothers: Women in the Struggle for America's Independence*. New York: Alfred A. Knopf, 2005.

Bohrer, Melissa Lukeman. *Glory, Passion and Principle: The Story of Eight Remarkable Women at the Core of the American Revolution*. New York: Atria Books, 2003.

Booth, Sally Smith. *The Women of '76*. New York: Hastings House, 1973.

Brandon, Ruth. *The Spiritualists: The Passion for the Occult in the 19ᵗʰ and 20ᵗʰ Centuries*. New York: Alfred A. Knopf, 1983.

Carter, Morris. *Isabella Stewart Gardner and Fenway Court*. Boston: Houghton Mifflin Company, 1925.

Christopher, Milbourne. *Mediums, Mystics and the Occult*. New York: Thomas Y. Crowell Company, 1975.

Cleary, Patricia. *Elizabeth Murray: A Woman's Pursuit of Independence in Eighteenth-Century America*. Amherst: University of Massachusetts Press, 2000.

Bibliography

Cohen, Daniel A. *Pillars of Salt, Monuments of Grace: New England Crime Literature and the Origins of American Pop Culture, 1674–1860*. New York: Oxford University Press, 1993.

Conant, Jennet. *A Covert Affair*. New York: Simon and Schuster, 2011.

Cook, Lauren J. "Katherine Nann, alias Naylor: A Life in Puritan Boston." *Historical Archaeology* 32, no. 1, Archaeologists as Storytellers (1998).

Cordingly, David. *Seafaring Women: Adventures of Pirate Queens, Female Stowaways and Sailors' Wives*. New York: Random House, 2007.

Cott, Nancy F. "Divorce and the Changing Status of Women in Eighteenth-Century Massachusetts." *William and Mary Quarterly* 33, no. 4 (October 1976).

Delgado, L. Anne. "Bawdy Technologies and the Birth of Ectoplasm." *Genders* 54 (2011).

Demos, John. *The Enemy Within: 2,000 Years of Witch-hunting in the Western World*. New York: Viking, 2008.

Evening Independent (St. Petersburg, FL). "Socialite Charged with Murder, Weeping Girl Admits Slaying." October 5, 1962.

———. "Suzanne Clift Has Baby; She Slew Lover." June 4, 1963, 3A.

Finison, Lorenz J. *Boston's Cycling Craze, 1880–1900*. Amherst: University of Massachusetts Press, 2013.

Garvey, Ellen Gruber. "Reframing the Bicycle: Advertising-Supported Magazines and Scorching Women." *American Quarterly* 47, no. 1 (March 1995).

Gerdes, Louise, ed. *Serial Killers*. Contemporary Issues Companion. San Diego, CA: Greenhaven Press, Inc., 2000.

Grant De Pauw, Linda. *Seafaring Women*. Boston: Houghton Mifflin, 1982.

Hall, David D., ed. *Witch Hunting in 17th Century New England: A Documentary History, 1638–1692*. Boston, MA: Northeastern University Press, 1991.

Heck, Dana B., and Joseph F. Balicki. "Katherine Naylor's 'House of Office': A Seventeenth-Century Privy." *Historical Archaeology* 32, no. 3. Perspectives on the Archaeology of Colonial Boston: The Archaeology of the Central Artery/Tunnel Project, Boston, MA (1998).

Hersey, Frank W.C. "The Misfortunes of Dorcas Griffiths." December 1937 Meeting of the Massachusetts Historical Society.

Hopkins, Caitlin G.D. "Enemies to Their Country." Vast Public Indifference. Blog. October 28, 2009.

Horton, James Oliver, and Lois E. Horton. *Black Bostonians*. New York: Holmes & Meier Publishers, Inc., 1979.

Hutcheson, Maud MacDonald. "Mercy Warren, 1728–1814." *William and Mary Quarterly* 10, no. 3 (July 1953): 378–402.

Irvin, Benjamin. *Samuel Adams: Son of Liberty, Father of Revolution*. New York: Oxford University Press, 2002.

Kalush, William, and Larry Sloman. *The Secret Life of Houdini: The Making of America's First Superhero*. New York: Atria Books, 2006.

Kastner, Joseph. "Long Before Furs, It Was Feathers That Stirred Reformist Ire." *Smithsonian* (July 1994).

Knickerbocker News (Albany, NY). "Can't Recall Fatal Shot, Boston Debutante Says." February 12, 1963, 1.

Knoblock, Glenn A. *The American Clipper Ship, 1845–1920: A Comprehensive History with a Listing of Builders and Their Ships*. Jefferson, NC: McFarland Publishing, 2014.

Kruh, David. "Little Known History Behind Old Howard." *Boston Globe*, February 2, 2002.

Leahy, Christopher W. *The Nature of Massachusetts*. Reading, MA: Addison Wesley, 1996.

Leonard, Todd Jay. *Talking to the Other Side: A History of Modern Spiritualism and Mediumship*. Lincoln, NE: iUniverse, 2005.

Lewis, Ann-Eliza H., ed. *Highway to the Past: The Archaeology of Boston's Big Dig*. Boston: Massachusetts Historical Commission, 2001.

Loewenberg, Bert James, and Ruth Bogin. *Black Women in Nineteenth Century American Life*. University Park: Pennsylvania State University Press, 1976.

Marks, Patricia. *Bicycles, Bangs and Bloomers: The New Woman in the Popular Press*. Lexington: University Press of Kentucky, 1990.

Mason, Kathy S. "Out of Fashion: Harriet Hemenway and the Audubon Society, 1896–1905." *The Historian* (January 2001).

Miami News. "Boston Killing: Suzy, Lawyer Plan Defense." October 7, 1962, 1A.

Mitchell, John H. "The Mothers of Conservation." *Sanctuary: The Journal of the Massachusetts Audubon Society* (January/February 1996).

Morgenroth, Lynda. *Boston Firsts: 40 Feats of Innovation and Invention That Happened First in Boston and Helped Make America Great*. Boston: Beacon Press, 2006.

Morrison, Anthony, and Nancy Lusignan Schultz, eds. *Salem: Place, Myth and Memory*. Boston: Northeastern University Press, 2004.

National Women's History Museum. "Sarah Remond (1826–1894)." www. nwhm.org/education-resources/biography/biographies/sarah-remond.

Negri, Gloria. "Shy Suzanne Clift Deeply in Love with Brentani, Stepfather Says." *Boston Globe*, October 6, 1962, 1.

New York Times. "Lady with Desire to Run Crashed Marathon." April 23, 1967.

Nicholls, Steve. *Paradise Found: Nature in America at the Time of Discovery*. Chicago: University of Chicago Press, 2009.

Norton, Mary Beth. *Liberty's Daughters: The Revolutionary Experience of American Women, 1750–1800.* Boston: Little, Brown and Company, 1980.

Oreovicz, Cheryl Z. "Legacy Profile: Mercy Otis Warren (1728–1814)." *Legacy* 13, no. 1 (1996).

O'Toole, James M., and David Quigley, eds. *Boston's Histories: Essays in Honor of Thomas H. O'Connor.* Boston: Northeastern University Press, 2004.

Pittsburgh Post-Gazette. "Boston Post-Deb Slayer Released on Probation." February 13, 1963, 1.

Porter, Dorothy Burnett. "The Remonds of Salem, Massachusetts: A Nineteenth-Century Family Revisited." *The Society* (1986).

Price, Jennifer. *Flight Maps: Adventures with Nature in Modern America.* New York: Basic Books, 1999.

Sarkela, Sandra J. "Freedom's Call: The Persuasive Power of Mercy Otis Warren's Dramatic Sketches, 1772–1775." *Early American Literature* 44, no. 3 (n.d.).

Schechter, Harold. *Fatal: The Poisonous Life of a Female Serial Killer.* New York: Pocket Books, 2003.

Schenectady Gazette. "Suzanne Clift Refuses to Reply in Court to Charge of Murder." November 28, 1962, 2.

Shand-Tuccci, Douglass. *The Art of Scandal: The Life and Times of Isabella Stewart Gardner.* New York: HarperCollins, 1997.

Shapiro, Laura. *Julia Child: A Life.* New York: Viking Adult, 2007.

Shatwell, Justin. "Boston Lighthouse Keeper Sally Snowman." *Yankee Magazine,* July 2009.

Simons, D. Brenton. *Witches, Rakes and Rogues: True Stories of Scam, Scandal, Murder and Mayhem in Boston, 1630–1775.* N.p.: Commonwealth Editions, 2005.

Snowman, Sally P., and James G. Thomson. *Boston Light: A Historical Perspective.* Plymouth, MA: Snowman Learning Center, 1999.

Souder, William. "How Two Women Ended the Deadly Feather Trade." *Smithsonian Magazine,* March 2013.

Spitz, Bob. *Dearie: The Remarkable Life of Julia Child.* New York: Random House, 2012.

Stashower, Daniel. "Mina Crandon and Harry Houdini: The Medium and the Magician." *American History* (August 1999).

Stevens, Peter F. *Notorious and Notable New Englanders.* Camden, ME: Down East Books, 1997.

Stuart, Nancy Rubin. "Conscience of the Revolution." *American History* (August 2008).

Sunday Herald (Bridgeport, CT). "Clift Denies She Intended to Kill Boy Friend. He Didn't Want Baby, She Testifies." February 10, 1963, 2.

Switzer, Kathrine. *Marathon Woman.* New York: Carroll & Graf Publishers, 2007.

Telegraph (Nashua, NH). "Miss Clift Undergoing Treatment." February 13, 1963, 3.

Venet, Wendy Hammond. *Neither Ballots Nor Bullets: Women Abolitionists and the Civil War.* Charlottesville: University Press of Virginia, 1991.

Weales, Gerald. "The Quality of Mercy, or Mrs. Warren's Profession." *Georgia Review* 33, no. 4 (Winter 1979).

Young, Philip. *Revolutionary Ladies.* New York: Alfred A. Knopf, 1977.

Zagarri, Rosemarie. *A Women's Dilemma: Mercy Otis Warren and the American Revolution.* Wheeling, IL: Harlen Davidson, 1995.

Zheutlin, Peter. *Around the World on Two Wheels.* New York: Citadel Press Books, 2007.

———. "Chasing Annie." *Bicycling Magazine*, May 2005.

Index

Index

U

United States Coast Guard 129, 130, 131
United States Coast Guard Auxiliary 129

W

Wall, George 53
Wall, Rachel 53, 54, 55, 56
Warren, James 28
Warren, Mercy Otis 27, 28, 29, 30,
 31, 32
Washington, Booker T. 96
West Barnstable, Cape Cod,
 Massachusetts 27
West End, Boston 70, 73
Weymouth, Massachusetts 128
WGBH-Boston 116
Wheelwright family 20
Whistler, James MacNeill 86, 88, 92
witchcraft 13, 16
Writs of Assistance 27, 42

About the Author

*D*ina Vargo has been a lover of history and tricorn hats since dressing up at the age of six as Betsy Ross for our nation's bicentennial. After receiving her BA in fine arts from the University of Pittsburgh, she worked for the Pittsburgh History & Landmarks Foundation and as a part-time archivist for the Rivers of Steel National Heritage Area. Dina also holds an MPA in public administration from the University of Pittsburgh. After moving to the Boston area, she became a docent for Boston By Foot, where she developed an interest for writing off-beat walking tours. She currently resides in Salem, Massachusetts, where she

Photo by Caitlin M. Fortin.

practices witchcraft only if the Steelers are playing. Her next project is to train for whatever marathon Kathrine Switzer and 261 Fearless crew are doing next.

Visit us at
www.historypress.net
....
This title is also available as an e-book